MANAGING YOURSELF

✓ THE CHECKLIST SERIES

MANAGING YOURSELF

First published in Great Britain in 2013 by
Profile Books Ltd
3a Exmouth House
Pine Street
Exmouth Market
London EC1R 0JH
www.profilebooks.com

10 9 8 7 6 5 4 3 2 1

A CIP catalogue record for this book is available from the British Library.

ISBN: 978 1 78125 145 4
eISBN: 978 1 84765 976 7

Text design by sue@lambledesign.demon.co.uk

Typeset in Helvetica by MacGuru Ltd
info@macguru.org.uk

Printed and bound in Britain by Bell & Bain Ltd

The diagram on pages 54 and 115 is adapted from the grief cycle model first published in *On Death and Dying* (1969) by Elisabeth Kubler-Ross. The original model has been applied here to the management of change.

All reasonable efforts have been made to obtain permission to reproduce copyright material. Any omissions or errors of attribution are unintentional and will be corrected in future printings following notification in writing to the publisher.

About the checklist series

Management can be a daunting task. Managers are expected to provide direction, foster commitment, facilitate change and achieve results through the efficient, creative and responsible deployment of people and other resources. On top of that, managers have to manage themselves and develop their own personal skills. Just keeping up is a challenge – and we cannot be experts in everything.

The checklists in this series have been developed over many years by the Chartered Management Institute (CMI) to meet this challenge by addressing the main issues that managers can expect to face during their career. Each checklist distils good practice from industry to provide a clear and straightforward overview of a specific topic or activity, and has been reviewed by CMI's Subject Matter Experts Panel to reflect new research and changes in working life.

The series is designed both for managers who need an introduction to unfamiliar topics, and for those who want to refresh their understanding of the salient points. In more specialised areas – for example, financial management – checklists can also enable the generalist manager to work more effectively with experts, or to delegate more effectively to a subordinate.

Why is the checklist format useful? Checklists provide a logical, structured framework to help professional managers deal with an increasingly complex workplace – they help shape our thoughts and save us from being confused by too much information. At the same time, checklists help us to make good use of what we already know. They help us to remember things and prevent us from forgetting something important. Thus, no matter how expert we may already be, using checklists can improve outcomes and give us the confidence to manage more effectively, and to get the job done.

About this book

Managing Yourself is aimed at anyone who wants to further their career as a manager. Using a combination of action-oriented checklists and handy short summaries of the ideas of seminal management thinkers, it will guide you past the pitfalls that beset even experienced managers. With checklists on how to develop your career and how to deal with crises, such as redundancy and choosing a second career, right through to planning your retirement, this concise and indispensable handbook will also help you master crucial skills such as problem-solving, networking and time management.

Contents

Developing yourself

Introduction

About one in five managers in the UK have no formal training in management: perhaps you are one of them. You may have reached a managerial position because you performed well in a specialist role, but *the skills that got you here are not the skills you can rely upon to take your career forward.* Knowing that few managers are trained for the role, it may not surprise you that in a recent survey by the Chartered Management Institute (CMI), 43% of employees in the UK considered their line managers to be ineffective or highly ineffective. If you are to deliver the desired outcomes, you owe it to those who report to you to learn new skills – and you will gain more respect from your team if you can focus, motivate and enable their best possible performance.

You also owe it to your employer to continuously develop yourself as a manager. In fact CMI evidence shows that investing in management and leadership development can lead to a 32% increase in people performance and a 23% increase in organisational performance.

Most of all, you owe it to yourself. Investing in your skills as a manager will give you greater confidence to deal with difficult or unfamiliar situations, and by overcoming problems you will achieve greater capability and satisfaction in your work.

The many opportunities and challenges you will face over time at work are compounded by the fact that 'careers' are no longer linear and predictable. Preparing for this is an important and individual matter. Of course employers have a contribution to make, and will benefit from your personal development and capability, but increasingly you can and must take responsibility for yourself.

You need to know yourself well and constantly review what you are learning. You can stretch yourself by seeking wider experience and skills at every stage, and being ready to learn from the situations you are in and the people you are with. And you need to learn how to sustain physical and emotional resilience so that you can handle stressful situations for yourself and for others. Looking after yourself is a continuing priority.

By seeing your development as a life-long undertaking, you will be able to give continuous commitment to it. In the process your own values will become clear, helping you to make the right decisions in the right way. You will be confident about what you know and humble about what you don't, and therefore able to be yourself. All this will support you as you manage your own career.

Improving all these skills will not always lead naturally to career advancement. You will also need to know how to 'manage upwards' – in other words, how to manage your boss. In a rapidly changing work environment you need to market yourself to take advantage of the opportunities, using your networks and presenting yourself effectively.

The message is clear – if you wish to lead and manage others, you need to know how to manage yourself.

Dame Mary Marsh
Founding Director, Clore Social Leadership Programme

Starting a new job

Starting a new job may imply that:

- an existing employee has been appointed to fill a vacancy in an existing or newly created job
- an individual has joined an organisation to fill a vacancy in an existing job or to assume the responsibilities of a newly created position.

This checklist focuses on the latter.

Starting a new job is an exciting but testing time when you will face many new challenges. While you may be justifiably proud of yourself for having completed the application process successfully and secured the position you wanted, this is not a time to rest on your laurels. Thinking about how you will approach the first few days and weeks in your new job and planning ahead for any potential issues you will face will help you to:

- reduce your stress levels
- become productive more quickly
- be accepted by new colleagues more quickly
- prepare for the cultural differences in your new organisation
- significantly reduce the potential for embarrassment which can arise in a new situation.

This checklist outlines practical steps which can be taken before you take up your new position and during the first few days in the job. Success depends not just on how you handle the first day with your new employer but on how you prepare in advance, even before you leave your current job. This checklist should also be helpful to organisations employing new starters.

Action checklist

1 Act positively before you leave your present job

Make sure that you sort out issues such as pension arrangements, private health insurance and your P45 with your HR or personnel department before you leave. Return any company property you have – badges and passes, computer equipment and mobile phones, for example. If you have received funding for qualifications or training, check whether you will be required to repay some or all of this. Does your contract of employment include any clauses restricting your movements or actions in the future?

2 Consider the implications of the new job for your work–life balance

Recognise that, whatever the level of the job, there will be a 'settling in' period during which extra focus and concentration will be required. The balance between your private and working lives may change, if only for a certain length of time, and your partners and family members will be affected. It is preferable to discuss this in advance to avoid or minimise any potential problems. Think too about any additional commitments you have outside work – leisure activities or voluntary work, for example – and decide whether any adjustments or temporary changes will be needed.

3 Research the background of your new employer

You will no doubt have carried out research into your new employer before your interview. Recognise that the more you know about the organisation you will be working for, the easier it will be for you to fit in during the initial period in your new job. Digest any documentation you have been given and find out what you can from company reports, corporate websites or industry publications.

Seek to identify:

- your new employer's competitors
- their relative degree of success or failure
- the basis on which they compete (such as price, quality, or service) or are protected from competition (because of location or access to raw materials, for example).

If you are new to the sector, consider how you can best familiarise yourself with it and acquire some knowledge of the terminology used. Remember that the people with whom you will be working may assume that you are familiar with their jargon. Try to get ahead of the game.

Find out anything you can about the culture of the organisation, the people with whom you will be working, the structure within which they work and the reputation of the unit which you will be joining. If you know anyone who is already employed by the organisation, glean what you can by talking to them.

Consider what you have discovered and its implications for a newcomer. Identify what you still need to know and resolve to take a proactive approach to gathering this information once you have started your new job. This will give you the advantage that comes from being well informed and enable you to impress your colleagues with your willingness to learn and work.

4 Make a good first impression

Check the joining instructions you have been given – where and when you are expected and whom you should report to. Make sure that you have familiarised yourself with the route to work and know how long it will take you to get there, making allowance for rush-hour traffic, if necessary. Dress appropriately, be friendly to everyone, take a lively interest in what you are told and show enthusiasm.

5 Take full advantage of induction programmes

The induction programme organised by your new employer should provide you with the information you need to do your job, as well as an understanding of organisational aims, objectives and operating procedures. Be prepared to listen and learn and don't be afraid to ask lots of questions. Take notes and keep them for future reference. If information is not provided, you will need to find it yourself, or ask for it. One place to start would be the staff handbook or organisational intranet, if there is one.

Recognise that you need to be clear about:

- the purpose of the unit you have joined
- the purpose of your new job
- your responsibilities
- your authority
- the structure of the unit
- the unit's place in the structure of the organisation
- who you report to and your boss's requirements
- who, if anyone, reports to you
- as much as possible about the culture and values of the unit and of the organisation.

6 Make sure you are clear about practical matters

These include day-to-day working practices as well as more long-term matters and include:

- start and finish times
- coffee, tea and lunch arrangements
- the use of facilities such as telephone, email and internet access for personal matters
- payment of wages and salaries
- holiday entitlements and procedures for booking leave
- pension arrangements

- performance appraisal or performance management programmes
- flexible working options
- additional employee benefits, such as private healthcare
- trade unions recognised by the organisation
- training and development opportunities.

What you need to know may range from the obviously important to the apparently trivial, but if it helps you fit in, become accepted and begin to do your new job more quickly, it is worth knowing. This may be even more important if you have been appointed to a newly created position.

7 Investigate the background if your job is newly created

Find out whether the job to which you have been appointed is a new one and if so, try to discover why it was created. Was it to solve a problem and if so, what was the problem? Was it to cope with expansion in activity and if so, what caused that expansion? Find out what the context of the newly created job is – what future plans there are for it and, most of all, what expectations there will be of you as the newly appointed post holder. Is the job unique in the organisation or are there others like it? Try to identify which of your characteristics and skills led to you being selected for the post – these will almost certainly provide the criteria against which your performance will be judged.

8 Consider what behaviour is appropriate

Remember that you are the newcomer and that your behaviour will be the focus of some attention, particularly if your new role requires you to manage or supervise others. Be yourself but leave yourself some room for manoeuvre in the light of what you may discover over the first two or three weeks in your new job.

Keep your eyes open. You will notice things in the first few weeks that you will soon come to take for granted. These may be things that you will wish to change later. Ask about them if you wish, but be careful not to start criticising practices in your new organisation too soon.

Reserve your position until you see how the land lies. Remember that it may not be easy to retract after speaking or acting too hastily. Be polite to everyone and offer help where appropriate, but even when offering help, don't allow yourself to act in an excessively assertive way.

9 Build relationships

Your relationships with your immediate colleagues, your boss and your team will be critical for your success in your new role. Seek out those who are best placed to help you find your way around the organisation and ask for their assistance. Don't limit your contacts to your immediate department – interacting with others from across the organisation will help you to gain a better understanding of the organisation as a whole and how your role fits within it. Take advantage of meetings and any social activities that are organised to establish contacts with colleagues from other departments, especially if their work has some bearing on your role.

10 Be prepared for that bewildered feeling

You will meet a lot of people and have many new processes to learn in your first days and weeks in a new job. The challenges can range from getting to grips with your job to finding out how to use a different kind of photocopier. Understand that it is natural to feel disoriented or even overwhelmed to start with. Most people don't feel fully comfortable in their new job for at least six months, so don't worry too much if you still feel at sea after only a couple of days.

11 Don't panic if the new job doesn't immediately meet expectations

The first weeks in a new job can vary tremendously. They may be very busy and pressured, making you feel that you have been thrown in at the deep end, or progress may seem frustratingly slow, as you are provided with lots of orientation material but feel you are not yet being given the opportunity to show what you can do. You may feel that you immediately get on well with your colleagues, or you may find them unfriendly and unapproachable, leaving you feeling isolated and uncomfortable. You may be receiving appreciation and recognition for your efforts, or you may suspect that your performance is not meeting with approval.

Don't jump to the conclusion that the move has been a mistake or take a hasty decision to resign. Give yourself time to settle in and your colleagues time to get used to you. If things are so bad that you do consider resigning, bear in mind that it is normally easier to find a job when you are in employment. Work to build good working relationships with your colleagues. Take every opportunity to demonstrate your willingness to learn and to make a contribution.

If problems persist or the role is not measuring up to the expectations you had of it, discuss your concerns with your line manager or mentor and seek to iron out any misconceptions or misunderstandings. If you are subject to a probationary period, it is advisable to raise any issues or misgivings you have before this comes to an end.

12 Set your objectives and plan for the future

It is important to consider what you want to get out of a new job and to set objectives for what you want to achieve. Set realistic and achievable goals, define what success will look like and start to develop plans for achieving them. Decide what your priorities are and start to gather the knowledge and develop the relationships that will help you to achieve them. Consider also what training or development you will need to help you develop the skills and competences required in your new role.

As a manager you should avoid:

- forming or being drawn into alliances too quickly
- being over-assertive or over-familiar with new colleagues
- trying to take the lead in discussions, formal or informal
- taking on too much in an effort to curry favour with others or prove yourself
- being too quick to suggest a social outing with colleagues
- boasting about your previous achievements
- making comparisons between your former employer and your new one
- taking decisions or expressing opinions that you may regret later.

New joiner: fitting in and getting on

Fitting in is about learning to function well within the social and cultural norms of the organisation, finding your place, being accepted and gaining the respect of colleagues. It involves building personal relationships and networks, and adapting to the culture and working environment of the organisation.

Getting on is about carrying out your job role effectively, meeting your objectives and making a positive contribution to the purpose and goals of the organisation.

The first weeks and months in a new job play a vital role in laying the foundations for personal achievement and success in a new organisation. However, starting a new job as a manager can be a challenging time – there are new people to meet, new skills to learn and new tasks to tackle. Your skills and abilities will be stretched as you face new challenges and opportunities. This checklist is intended to help managers starting a job in a new organisation to be aware of the issues they need to consider and to develop a strategy for success. It looks at how to fit into the organisation, develop relationships and demonstrate that you can fulfil the responsibilities you have been given.

Action checklist

1 Consider your approach

When starting out in a new job, it is important to find the right balance between confidence in your own abilities and your need to learn. Overconfidence can be seen as arrogance and cause you to forfeit the goodwill and cooperation of your colleagues. Excessive humility, on the other hand, may lead people to doubt your abilities. Try to strike a balance between the two, presenting yourself as confident but willing to listen and learn.

2 Get to grips with your job role

Your first priority should be to understand the job you have been appointed to do and what is expected of you. Make sure you are clear about your responsibilities, reporting lines and the extent and boundaries of your authority. Find out what systems, structures, processes and procedures are in place. Discuss and, if necessary, renegotiate objectives and performance measures for your work with your line manager. Take full advantage of any induction programmes which are arranged for you and don't be afraid to ask questions if you need clarification or further information. Start by familiarising yourself with the work of your team or department and how it operates on a day-to-day basis.

3 Use your new role for change

Your new role gives you the opportunity to introduce change and improvements – to some extent this will be expected. Don't rush into making changes without understanding the situation fully, but from the outset start to think about the vision you have for your role and to develop goals for yourself and your team. Prioritise the changes you want to make and decide who you need to consult with. Discuss your ideas with all those concerned before going ahead.

4 Build relationships

The relationships you build are vital to your success in the organisation. You need to balance your concern for 'getting the job done' with building relationships with your colleagues. Don't become so engrossed in your personal tasks that you neglect people and become insensitive to your colleagues. Focus on getting to know your team and your boss, but don't neglect wider organisational contacts and networks, Remember that relationships take time and patience. Be prepared to join in with any social events – this will give you a wider feel for the organisation and help you to get to know others and others to get to know you.

5 Look out for key contacts

Start early on to identify key people – those you will need to influence if you are to achieve your objectives and reap benefits for the organisation and yourself. It is helpful to have one-to-one meetings with such people, so that you can find out about their job roles and their priorities and understand how to gain their support for any changes and new initiatives you wish to introduce. Consider also finding a suitable mentor within the organisation. A mentoring relationship can be extremely helpful at any stage, but newly appointed managers may find it especially useful in helping them gain insight into organisational norms – management styles, culture and networks.

6 Consider organisational culture

Different organisations have different ways of doing things. Carrying on in your usual manner may not sit well with colleagues in your new organisation and in some cases may cause offence. Be aware of this and keep your eyes open for clues about 'how things are done around here'. It's also important to realise that official organisational culture and values may not reflect how things actually work in practice. If you are not sure about how to proceed, ask your immediate colleagues for advice.

Be flexible and think through which aspects of your personal style or working practices you need to adjust. This will help you to gain acceptance and become integrated. However, don't feel that you have to put on an act or compromise the real you. The key is to find a balance between adapting to the organisation and maintaining enough of your personal identity to be able to make a difference.

7 Be aware of informal organisational structures

Every organisation has informal power structures which operate independently and bypass official structures and communication channels. Keep your eyes open for evidence of how both formal and informal structures are operating within your new organisation, and use your developing network of contacts and allies to help you understand how and when to make best use of formal and informal channels.

8 Think about values

As you have accepted the job, you will most likely be broadly in sympathy with the aims and purpose of the organisation. Nonetheless, it is helpful to consider the fit between organisational values and your own personal values. Many organisations have a statement of values, but these may or may not reflect reality. Careful observation of how people behave and what they do or don't do will help you to assess the actual as opposed to the stated values. Decide what you stand for personally and consider the extent to which you can align yourself with organisational values without compromising your personal beliefs. Think too about how you can demonstrate these values in your personal behaviour and relationships.

9 Challenge appropriately

While it is important to do what you can to fit in with your new colleagues, you have been appointed for the skills, knowledge and expertise you can offer, so don't feel that you have to become an 'organisational clone'. You bring a fresh eye to the business and will have a valid contribution to make. The important thing is to do this appropriately. Make sure you understand the reasons things are done as they are before challenging them – there may be valid legal or operational reasons. On the other hand, there may be more effective ways of getting the job done and a newcomer may be in a position to ask questions. Always try to take a constructive approach, rather than being negative and critical.

10 Demonstrate credibility

Look out for early opportunities to reassure those who appointed you that they have picked the right person for the job. Try to identify a simple task or improvement which can be achieved within your first few weeks and give you an 'early win'. This will help to give you and your colleagues confidence in your abilities and give you time to tackle more complex tasks and issues in the future.

11 Ask for feedback and reflect on progress

Feedback may be provided through an organisational appraisal or performance management system, but more frequent feedback from your line manager and colleagues will help you adapt to a new situation. Ask them how you are doing and consider requesting regular meetings to discuss progress. Take time to reflect on what you have achieved and what your next priorities should be. Don't write yourself off if you make mistakes, but accept this as part of the learning curve. Do what you can to put things right, resolve to learn from the experience and move on. Bear in mind, however, that while mistakes may be accepted in the early days, they may be viewed less favourably as time goes on and you will be expected to have found your feet and become effective in your job role.

12 Make the most of learning and development opportunities

As you settle into your new role, assess your strengths and weaknesses and consider whether there are any specific areas where personal development is needed. Find out how learning and development are handled in the organisation. Is there an annual review process for identifying development needs? Are coaching and/or mentoring relationships available? Take advantage of formal and informal learning opportunities – these need not necessarily be expensive or time-consuming.

13 Keep an eye on the bigger picture

Take an organisation-wide view of your work, and find out how your department or project fits within the overall aims and purpose of the organisation. Arrange meetings with colleagues to find out what they do and how they operate. Explore the environment within which the organisation operates as well, especially if you are working in an industry sector which is unfamiliar to you. Who are the organisation's major stakeholders – customers and suppliers, for example? Who are the major competitors? What local, national and international factors affect the organisation? Talking to people inside and outside the organisation, reading the trade press, visiting key industry web portals, subscribing to an online news feed or joining relevant online communities are all ways to develop your knowledge.

14 Take care of yourself

Starting a new job is a stressful experience. Meeting people and adapting to new situations can be very tiring. Realise that you may need to make adjustments to your schedule to maintain your physical and mental health while you adapt to your new role. While you will be keen to work hard and make a good impression, resist the temptation to work excessive hours and wear yourself out. Consider whether you need to manage expectations in this area and start as you mean to go on. Make sure you eat well and get time for rest and relaxation.

As a manager you should avoid:

- riding roughshod over established practices and norms
- comparing the new organisation with one where you worked previously
- saying 'When I worked at x, we did it this way'
- adopting a know-it-all approach
- compromising personal integrity in order to fit in

- getting bogged down in everyday routine tasks
- spending too much time organising benefits such as company car, mobile phones or medical insurance
- losing sight of the bigger picture
- failing to learn from mistakes.

New joiner: handling workplace relationships

A new joiner is someone who has recently become employed in an organisation for which they haven't previously worked.

This checklist is intended for junior managers who have recently joined an organisation and are undertaking their first managerial role. It considers the important role that your relationships with your boss, your peers, and your team play in the process of integration, and outlines steps which can help to ensure success in your new workplace and your new role.

Joining an organisation can be a daunting prospect, and becoming a first-time manager presents many new challenges. As a manager, you will find that your team will look to you for guidance, and your boss will look to you for results. Your colleagues play a significant part in your success as a new manager, as you can draw on their knowledge and experience of the organisation to help you to fit in. It is well worth taking the time, therefore, to work out a strategy for developing your relationships with those closest to you. You may find them to be a welcoming group of people who will happily give you all the support you need to fit in. Alternatively, you may find that this is not the case and this will make the integration process more challenging.

Gaining support, acceptance and trust from your new colleagues will take time. However, by establishing solid working relationships from the outset, you will receive the support, help and information which will prove invaluable to you as you orient yourself within your new position and validate yourself as a manager.

Action checklist

1 Build good working relationships

In the early days, your effectiveness within your new role largely depends upon those around you. Therefore it is in your best interest to develop a good working relationship with your boss, your team and your peers by building trust and rapport from the start. Entering a close community can feel quite daunting. Look for things that you have in common and try to build on these. Ask open questions, listen carefully and show interest in the answers. It may be appropriate to offer help on specific projects that are being run or to ask for others' input on something you are planning to do. Relationships take time to build, but once you have demonstrated competence and credibility to your boss, your peers and your team, you are on the path to gaining their trust and acceptance.

2 Build a good working relationship with your boss

Aim to develop a good working relationship with your boss, even if they are not the type of person you would make your personal friend. Ensure that you manage any disagreements or differences of opinion that arise in a respectful way. Your effectiveness depends on your boss's participation, at least until you have established credibility in your own right within the organisation.

Your boss has a key role to play in:

- identifying what you need to learn to get the job done well and methods by which this learning could be acquired

- explaining and interpreting the organisation's social conventions, including the mannerisms, dress codes and ways of speaking that are acceptable for someone in your position, and the leeway that is permitted in carrying out the role

- explaining and interpreting the organisation's norms for business success

- demonstrating the values of the organisation and the department

- helping you develop a 'map of the territory' that sufficiently matches those that longer-serving members carry

- supporting you in letting go of past roles, and in some cases unlearning lessons learned in your previous organisation.

3 Find out where your role fits within the overall organisational hierarchy

One of the things which newcomers to an organisation find most difficult is to understand the relationships, reporting lines and transfer of knowledge across the organisation. The formal organisation chart is unlikely to give a full picture of how things are actually done. You need to know which members of your peer group have a direct/indirect interest in, or impact on, the work that you have been employed to do. There may be people in the organisation who have a powerful but indirect bearing on your work. These are likely to be the information gatherers and networkers. They can be difficult to identify, but by asking around you will be able to find out who they are. Get to know them and help them get to know you.

Sometimes conflicts arise where there are unclear boundaries, or overlaps and duplications, between job roles. These greying lines of responsibility are particularly likely to occur if your new role has arisen as a result of a reorganisation and things are still in a state of flux. Initiate collaborative conversations with people as soon as you become aware of potential conflicts of interest so that you can attempt to iron these out.

It is important that you gain an understanding of the culture of the organisation as it will largely govern how you fulfil your role. It will have an impact on your behaviour and will influence your decision-making.

4 Demonstrate that you have what it takes to be a successful manager

People who do well when joining an organisation tend to have certain characteristics in common. They:

- are direct and forceful and assert themselves in an effective way
- recognise and use their intuition
- are open to new experiences
- can cope in conditions of uncertainty
- develop three to five power bases from which to influence (positional, expert, personal, resource, association)
- learn quickly
- are oriented towards the future not the past.

These characteristics will help you to respect the organisation and its members, yet constructively challenge assumptions and ways of operating where necessary. If you are to manage your team effectively and satisfy your boss that you are able to carry out the role with which you have been tasked, you need to demonstrate the behaviours appropriate to your grade of management. They need to see that you have the intention and the capability to work in their best interests, and that you have credibility and visibility with the people who matter in the organisation.

5 Articulate exactly how you add value to both your team and your organisation's performance

You need to validate your role as a manager, answering questions such as: 'What am I going to contribute to the business?' and 'How will my experience contribute to the team's performance?' You were hired to get the job done. In the first instance, identify deliverables which are high-impact and low-risk and which you can work on as you get to know the organisation. Try to anticipate what your boss and your colleagues are looking for and provide solutions for them in advance of their request. It is trite but true to say that you should aim to bring solutions not problems.

It is not enough for you to be seen to be achieving results yourself. You are responsible for managing the work and performance of others, and thus need to prove to your boss that you can do this effectively. You may have inherited a team of people who have become demotivated and it may be difficult to re-engage them. Nevertheless, it is vital to act quickly to improve the situation.

6 Make changes sensitively

Understandably you will have your own ideas on how you are going to deliver your objectives and this may involve making changes to the status quo. If you are aiming to implement new processes and change the way your team works, the mix of people within it, or its sphere of operation, you need to present good reasons for doing so, so that people can understand. A consultative approach that takes the opinions and suggestions of team members into account is more likely to be accepted and to gain buy-in. If you do meet with resistance, especially if you are seeking to make significant changes to long-established processes, listen carefully to the concerns and objections of others, showing empathy and understanding, and aim to alleviate tension by clearly articulating how and why the business context makes the proposed changes necessary.

7 Broker discussions on how things are going within the team and its sphere of operation

Inevitably, issues and dilemmas that team members find difficult to resolve among themselves will arise and they may feel uncomfortable bringing these to you. With line manager responsibility, you need to be sensitive to the undercurrents that are part and parcel of the team's activities. If you sense something is not going as well as it might, it is your responsibility to bring it into the open for discussion and resolution. Equally, if things are going well, it is your role to recognise and give due praise to team members for good performance.

Remember to treat people with respect at all times, listening to their views and responding emphatically to their concerns. By listening to what is being said, and responding accordingly, your team will begin to trust you. The more they communicate with you, the better you will get to know them. From this more familiar standpoint, you are then able to make an accurate assessment of both your team's performance as a whole and the performance of individual team members.

8 Make time to have regular meetings with each member of your team

Even if you have regular team meetings, it is also important to schedule regular one-to-one meetings with your team members. This will ensure that:

- they receive personal feedback on their performance from you
- you can get to know them better
- you can discuss individual development needs
- you can also receive feedback from them on how you are doing.

Showing interest in individual as well as team progress is a powerful tool for keeping people motivated. Remember to listen to what is not said as much as what is said in meetings.

9 Listen to constructive feedback

As well as being accountable for your team and their development, you are accountable for your own development. Listening and responding to feedback you receive from your boss, your team and your peers will help you to achieve the objectives of the organisation, the team you are responsible for, and your own personal and professional development. Respond to any feedback you receive, both positive and negative, and use it to improve your performance, making the changes that are needed to help you make a sound contribution in your new managerial role.

As a manager you should avoid:

- failing to build sound working relationships with colleagues
- making changes without consulting with others or explaining the rationale behind them

- failing to respond to constructive feedback
- working independently, without the support, guidance and acceptance of those closest to you.

profile

Edgar Schein

Careers, culture and organisational learning

Introduction

Edgar Schein (b. 1928) pioneered the concept of corporate culture with his landmark book *Organizational Culture and Leadership* (1985), which sparked off much research into organisational culture. He also coined the now much-used phrases 'Psychological Contract' and 'Career Anchor'.

Life and career

Now the Sloan Fellows' Professor of Management Emeritus and Senior Lecturer at the MIT Sloan School of Management, Schein has had a long and distinguished academic career. He has made a strong contribution to the 'helping' professions, mainly in the areas of organisation development, career development and organisational culture. He received his PhD in social psychology from Harvard University, collaborated with Douglas McGregor at MIT and worked for many years at the National Training Laboratory.

Schein has extensively researched and written about the factors that influence individual and organisational performance. The main themes underlying his work are the identification of culture(s) in the organisation; the relationship between organisational culture and individual behaviour; and the importance of organisational culture for organisational learning.

McGregor invited Schein to MIT after the latter's post-war work on the repatriation of prisoners of war following the end of the Korean War. This strongly influenced Schein's career, and re-emerged forcefully in an article for *The Learning Organization* in 1999 on brainwashing and organisational persuasion techniques ('Empowerment, coercive persuasion and organizational learning: do they connect?', Vol. 6, No. 4, pp. 163–72).

Schein's thinking

Corporate culture

Early in his career, Schein found traditional approaches to understanding work behaviour and motivation both too simplistic to explain the range of experiences of individuals in organisations and too restrictive, as human and organisational needs vary widely from person to person, place to place and time to time. In *Organizational Culture and Leadership*, he became the first management theorist to define corporate culture and suggest ways in which culture is the dominant force within an organisation.

In his view, culture is a mix of many different factors, such as:

- observed behavioural regularities when people interact
- norms that evolve in working groups
- dominant values pushed by the organisation
- philosophy guiding the attitudes of senior management to staff and customers
- organisational rules, procedures and processes
- the feeling or climate that is conveyed without a word being spoken.

In *Organizational Culture and Leadership*, Schein defines culture as a pattern of basic assumptions, and discusses how these fall into five, often oppositional, categories:

1 **Humanity's relationship to nature** – some organisations seem to want to dominate the external environment, while others accept its domination.

2 **The nature of reality and truth** – the ways and means by which organisations arrive at the 'truth'.

3 **The nature of human nature** – some people seem to avoid work if they possibly can, while others embrace it as a way of fulfilling their potential, to both their own and the organisation's benefit.

4 **The nature of human activity** – a focus on the completion of tasks on the one hand, and on self-fulfilment and personal development on the other.

5 **The nature of human relationships** – some organisations seem to facilitate social interaction, while others regard it as an unnecessary distraction.

Organisational socialisation

Schein's thoughts on organisational socialisation were triggered when, after arriving at MIT, he asked McGregor for guidance in the form of previous outlines and notes for a course he was preparing. McGregor politely refused, saying there was no need to rely on history and that Schein should make up his own mind. This lesson in acclimatising to MIT led Schein to argue that companies should be conversant with their socialisation practices, and recognise the conflicts they can create for new recruits.

In his article 'Organizational socialisation and the profession of management' (*Sloan Management Review*, Fall 1988, pp. 53–65), Schein discusses how, when a new recruit enters an organisation, a process of socialisation – adaptation or 'fit' – takes place. He argues that this process has more to do with recruits' past experience and values than their qualifications or formal training.

Usually, Schein suggested, organisations create a series of events that work to undo the new recruit's old values to some extent, so that he or she is more open to learning new values. This process of 'undoing' or 'unfreezing' can be unpleasant, and its success may therefore depend upon either a recruit's strong motivation to endure it, or the organisation's perseverance in making recruits endure it. There are three basic responses to this socialisation process:

- **rebellion** – outright rejection of the organisation's norms and values
- **creative individualism** – selective adoption of key values and norms
- **conformity** – acceptance of the organisation's norms and values.

Noting similarities between brainwashing experienced by members of the armed forces captured during the Korean War and the socialisation of executives on programmes at MIT, Schein argues that many forms of organisational development involve restructuring and change, and have serious implications for the way people work and their relationship with management.

Schein likens such organisation development processes to a form of coercive persuasion, or brainwashing, giving people little choice but to abandon, for example, older norms and values that fit badly with the new learning. If we are in tune with the goals and values of the change this will not be a problem, but if we dislike the values, we are likely to disapprove of the 'brainwashing'. Schein concludes that, because the very concept of organisation involves some restriction of individual freedom to achieve a joint purpose, the concept of a continually learning, innovative organisation is something of a paradox, since creativity and learning are related to individual freedom and growth.

Organisational learning

Organisational learning, Schein considers, needs to be fast in order to cope with growing market pressures, yet it seems to be obstructed by a fear of, or anxiety about, facing change, particularly on the part of senior executives. This feeling is associated with reluctance to learn what is new because it appears too difficult or disruptive. Schein argues that only a new anxiety greater than the existing one can overcome this, and his 'anxiety 2' is the fear, shame or guilt associated with not learning anything new.

Schein emphasises the need for people to feel psychologically safe if change is to happen. Achieving organisational learning and transformation therefore depends upon creating a feeling of safety, and overcoming the negative effects of past incentives and past punishments – especially the latter. To learn, people need to feel motivated and free to try out new things.

Psychological contract and career anchors

In his book *Organizational Psychology*, Schein highlights a 'psychological contract' (attributing the original concept to Chris Argyris), which he defines as an unwritten set of expectations operating between employees and employing managers and others in an organisation. He stresses how essential it is that both parties' expectations of a contract should match if a long-term relationship that will benefit both parties is to develop.

Closely linked to the notion of the psychological contract is the concept of the career anchor, which describes a guiding force that influences individuals' career choices and is based on their self-perceptions. Schein proposes that, from their varying aspirations and motivations, individuals – perhaps unconsciously – develop one underlying career anchor, which they are unwilling to surrender. On the basis of 44 cases, he distinguishes career anchor groups such as technical/functional competence, managerial competence, creativity, security or stability and autonomy.

The three cultures of management

Rather than a single culture, Schein identifies three cultures (or communities of interest) within an organisation that often conflict rather than work in harmony:

- the **operator culture**, which evolves locally within organisations and within operational units

- the **engineering culture** of technicians in search of 'people-free' solutions

- the **executive culture**, which is focused on financial survival.

  For example, while the executive culture would require systems and reporting relationships for evidence that operations are on track, the engineering culture would attempt to design systems that cut across lines of control and the people manning these.

  In his article 'Three cultures of management: the key to organizational learning' (*Sloan Management Review*, Fall 1996, pp. 9–20), Schein suggests that, often, either operators assume executives and engineers do not understand their work needs and covertly do things in their own way, or executives or engineers assume a need for tighter control over operators and force them to follow policies and procedure manuals. In each case, there is no commonly understood plan and efficiency and effectiveness suffer.

  Schein stresses the need to take the concept of culture more seriously and accept how deeply embedded are the assumptions of executives, engineers and employees. He proposes that helping executives and engineers learn how to learn about, analyse and evolve their cultures may be central to organisational learning.

In perspective

Schein's work now spans over four decades and his great contribution has been in linking culture with individual development and growth, putting the accent on organisations as complex systems and on individuals as whole beings.

Schein was aware that the concept of corporate culture was no cure-all for ailing organisations. The fact, however, that culture is now generally recognised as a central factor for organisational change and development is largely attributable to his work.

New joiner: developing your network

Networking has become accepted as a term to describe the activities involved in building and maintaining formal and informal relationships. Networks may overlap; two people may belong to the same network but each will have contacts in other networks. Networks are not static – they evolve, expand and shrink according to the perceived needs and actions of the networkers.

There are three main types of network: personal, professional and organisational. The focus here is on organisational networking.

Establishing and developing a personal network within your organisation will give you a wider awareness of the context in which you are working, helping you to fulfil your job role, contribute to organisational objectives and achieve your personal goals more effectively. Relationships developed through networking can provide access to information, development opportunities and support. Ultimately they can enable you to become influential, gain promotion and develop your career.

It is important to plan ahead and to think about whom you should network actively with and which relationships will be beneficial to you. Time spent on networking may seem wasteful in the short term, but it will be worthwhile in the long term. Demonstrating that you can link into and add something to a network will enhance your organisational visibility and credibility, provide a source of feedback and social support, and help to improve your status within the organisation.

To network successfully, an awareness of relationships and of their potential value both to yourself and to other members of the group is crucial. Many people view networking with trepidation. This checklist aims to provide practical advice to help those new to an organisation start out on the process of getting connected.

Action checklist

1 Be approachable

If you come into an organisation and start by asking tough questions in a way which makes people uncomfortable, you run the risk of offending and alienating your colleagues.

It may well be necessary to shake things up, but you need to learn to do this in the right way and at the right time. Start by listening and being ready to receive feedback. Be open-minded, approachable and forthcoming.

2 Be aware that people will weigh you up

New joiners are often regarded warily to start with. Your colleagues will want to find out who you are and size you up before accepting you – all the more so, if you come in with a different style or way of operating to which they are not accustomed. Understand that this is a natural tendency, give people time and do what you can to help them get to know you.

3 Develop a reliable network

Rumour, gossip and the grapevine operation run parallel to formal organisational communications. You will need sources of information and support that are independent, reliable and non-manipulative. In relatively unknown territory, it is easy to be misled by unreliable or biased information or to take hasty action on the basis of something you have heard without checking the facts first. To avoid difficulties of this kind, take the time to assess who and what you can rely on to be truthful and accurate.

4 Build your networks across, down and up

Organisational cultures are rooted in personalities, their connections, interactions and ways of doing things – who knows whom, what goes on. It is not enough to establish connections at your own level in the organisation. You need to include people of all types and levels to really tap into the mindset of the organisation. Consider how much a driver, receptionist or a local union representative might know about what's going on and who's meeting whom. Usually a small number of people are the linchpins in the networks and everyone else is connected through them. Being new to the organisation you need to identify the 'connectors', as it is they who can introduce you to the wider network.

5 Get your network up and running

In building your network, you need to find enough support to enable you to swim as opposed to sink. People may assume that because you have the professional and technical skills to do the job you also have the connections, but you need to engage help from the start to get yourself linked up.

One way of doing this is to ask your immediate work colleagues to name those in the organisation who 'know everybody'. You will probably hear the same name or names repeated a number of times. These people are important not simply because of the number of people they know but because of the types of people they know. You have to judge whether they are busybodies or good connectors.

Good connectors span different domains – they have contacts in various groups and subgroups. By using their innate connecting skills they manage to bring these domains together. The skill of these natural networkers is not that they view all their contacts as friends, but that they see them as acquaintances with whom they seek to maintain a connection. Acquaintances represent a source of social power, and the more you have the more powerful you are. Natural networkers who have a wealth of these 'weak ties' can give you access to the people and information you need.

6 Remember the importance of relationships

Generally, people who are new to an organisation find it easier to form relationships if they are in a position to offer specific technical skills that other people need, such as legal skills. People coming into more generalist roles – working, for example, as change managers, – find it much harder to establish relationships. Their expertise is not necessarily required by others (and indeed may be resisted). You need to base your relationships around your organisational 'calling card' – what it is that makes you visible and what you are known for. Take time to think this through.

7 Maintain network development activity throughout your career

In a large organisation, it can take between nine and fifteen months to learn and understand how things work and to get to know enough people to manage your network effectively. This means that you need to work consciously on developing your network over a significant period of time. Once you feel comfortable in your new role you may lose the drive to maintain your relationships. If this happens, your network will weaken – this is a risky thing to allow, as you do not know when you will need to make use of it. Networks give you a good finger on the pulse and act as a source of ideas – you will need both of these to maintain your performance and your position in the organisation.

8 Establish networks in many worlds

Ask yourself how many worlds you belong to – you may have worked in several industry sectors, for example, or be a member of sports and social clubs. All of these are sources of information. Often, the ability to make connections across these worlds will pay dividends – a number of product innovations, for example, have come about because people have made a connection between two apparently different worlds. It is the same with relationships and ideas: different worldviews can be a source of inspiration.

9 Reciprocate by giving access to your networks

When you arrive in a new organisation, you bring your existing network connections with you. You are in a position to give those with whom you will now be developing relationships access to contacts that you have already established. Reciprocity is healthy. Don't be cagey or grudging about it – look for opportunities to exploit the contacts you have. You will probably be pleasantly surprised by the value that reciprocity brings.

10 Accept that feeling isolated is part of being new

Generally, people in organisations intend to be welcoming to newcomers but the fact is that most people are incredibly busy and may not recognise your needs as a new joiner. This is not for reasons of malice or rejection, but due to lack of time. It may be easy to become lonely or feel isolated. If you work actively at making connections this feeling is unlikely to last long.

As a manager you should avoid:

- spending time networking at the expense of delivering on the job – balance the two

- assuming that you will be successful without developing a network of contacts

- neglecting the networks of which you are already a part – you may need them in the future.

New joiner: making an impact

Making an impact is defined for the purpose of this checklist as obtaining wide recognition that what you are achieving is of benefit to the organisation and not just to your immediate sphere of operation. This implies gaining organisational visibility for your efforts in a way that adds to your standing within the organisation. With this in mind, the methods you use to make an impact need to be appropriately chosen and deployed.

In coming new to an organisation, it is important to make a positive impact quickly – that is, within three months, and sooner than that if possible. The way to make an impact is to prove that you are capable of quick delivery that improves business performance and brings people with you as you do it. You have to think radically but not rock the boat too much – quite a difficult balance to achieve.

It may come as a shock to realise that even though you have relevant experience that you expect will enable you to hit the ground running, this may not turn out to be the case – usually because you do not yet have the ability to apply the experience in the new context. This is a difficult situation to be in, especially if you come in at a senior level where you are working in a new area and trying to keep ahead of the game. At senior levels in particular you are highly visible in the organisation (or your part of it), and any mistakes you make are noticeable and potentially damaging. With all this in mind, you should recognise that newness is not an excuse for lack of impact.

Making an impact may help to set the stage for the way people will perceive you in the future. It can also give you confidence that you are on the right track in the new organisation and help integrate you into the fabric of the organisation.

What are the right conditions for making an impact? You need to:

- be in a job where you can make an impact – sometimes this may be difficult if there are boundaries or restrictions on your freedom of action or you are not the person setting the agenda
- have the skills to get people to recognise (as well as value) your contribution
- get people working on your side as you put your plans into action
- exhibit the 'right behaviours' as you strive to make your impact.

Action checklist

1 Link into the organisational navigation system rapidly

You need to be out and about, listening, learning and responding. Look happy and confident as you do this. Ask lots of questions and be willing to listen to the answers. Find out from people what they would consider doing to make a positive impact if they were in your role. Balance being consultative with acting quickly, effectively and decisively

Emotionally engaging leadership styles pay real dividends. If you can engage people as allies in your cause, create a sense of joint accomplishment, camaraderie and emotional attachment, tell it like it is and keep them informed about your plans, you will go a long way to making a positive impact and achieving delivery targets.

2 Engage your immediate work colleagues to help you deliver

You can't make an impact without actively involving other people in what you're trying to do. As well as engaging them emotionally, you need either to ask them to help you in specific ways or to give them an active part to play in your plans. Sharing a joint sense of pride in a job well done has more impact than achieving the task on your own.

3 Make an impact upwards as well as at your own level

If you are hoping for a long-term career in the organisation, you need to ensure that what you do is noticed by people higher up. You can do this in various ways, either directly or indirectly. Direct methods include getting yourself on an agenda to give a presentation on your plans or a progress report on what you have achieved. Indirect methods include writing pieces for any newsletters that circulate around the organisation and being quoted in the trade press. One caveat: you need to handle the politics of making an upward impact with care.

4 Make sure that your contribution is recognised

This means sharing your thoughts and making the right people aware of your contribution, but not being boastful or self-serving as you talk about the part you are playing in developing the business. Recognition comes in a number of different ways and you need to be clear about what form it takes in your new organisation.

5 Build patterns of success

Once you have made an initial impact, you cannot afford to rest on your laurels. You will have set expectations that you need to continue to meet. This can be demanding if you are relying on yourself and not delegating effectively or involving and encouraging others in supporting you. Making an impact through the skills of your people is a good way to build a pattern of success.

6 Help your stakeholders to see what you want them to see about you

People will look to see whether you are fulfilling the expectations they had of you when you were offered the job. What they want to find is that you are a person who can get the job done and bring people along with you while doing so. You need to be (not just act like) someone with personal integrity and the ability to survive. To be and do all this you need to look after yourself, know how to manage the stresses of the job and get help when you need it.

7 Remember your work is part of a larger scheme

In planning to make an impact through what you do, remember that your contribution has to dovetail with the overall scheme of things. Until you understand the part that you and your team play in the wider context, you are unlikely to be able to make a meaningful contribution (and thus impact) in your role.

8 Make an impact with the big picture rather than the detail

As a new member of the organisation you have the benefit of a fresh perspective. Endeavour to understand the situation you are planning to change at a 'big picture' level. Help others to see this big picture from a number of different angles and to generate with you a range of options for changes. It is easier to make a recognisable impact at the higher level than in the details.

9 Create a vision

Get energy and commitment behind your plans by creating a vision of what you are trying to achieve hand in hand with the people who will be helping you to attain your objectives. This needs to be a genuinely shared vision, not one which people feel they have to adopt because you hold the lead role. Delivering on a shared vision is a great way of making a positive organisational impact.

As a manager you should avoid:

- allowing past success in a previous role or organisation to make you overconfident or give you a sense of invincibility
- being closed to feedback about the impact you are making
- assuming that making an impact is a 'one-off' thing – it needs to be an ongoing process.

Succeeding as a new manager

A 'new manager' is the newly appointed holder of a post that entails responsibility for a team of people.

New managers may be people who have moved into their first management post, or people who have moved up to new levels of management responsibility. The relationship between manager and team will be a new one, even if the manager previously worked with the team as a colleague, or knew the team members through his or her work in another part of the same organisation.

The principles outlined here apply to anyone taking up a new management post.

Newly appointed managers are likely to face many challenges once they are in post. Most management or leadership roles involve managing and taking responsibility for the work and performance of others. Rather than focusing solely on tasks to be completed, new managers may be involved for the first time in setting targets, handling team workloads and ensuring that deadlines are met, or may be taking on a new level of responsibility for a department or functional area. They will need to build relationships, motivate their team and deal with any emotional issues that arise. There will be much to absorb and get used to during the first few weeks, and it may take two or three months to settle into the role.

Thinking about how to adjust and adapt to the new pressures, and identifying the main issues to focus on, will help the new manager to get to grips with the job as quickly as possible. By considering the best approach to take, and preparing for it carefully, the new manager should be able to feel confident of his or her future success. This checklist outlines the main issues managers should consider when taking up a new post.

Action checklist

1 Get it right before you start

After learning of and celebrating your new appointment, you need to try to estimate how much difference it will make to your life. Once you get to grips with your new role, you are likely to find that it takes more time and attention than your previous work required. Recognise that you will need support at home during a period in which you will be on a steep learning curve that may be stressful, as well as freedom from distractions so you can give full attention to your new responsibilities. From the start, and throughout the adjustment period, discuss the potential implications with your family or close friends. How will the change affect your relationships with your partner and family? Will it alter the patterns of life you are all accustomed to?

2 Find out about the job in advance

Find out all you can about:

- the organisation (if it is one you have not previously worked for)
- the unit or department where you will work
- your new job and the responsibilities involved
- the history of the position
- your new team members, if you don't already know them.

Don't prejudge what you're going to find in your new job, or let your thinking be limited by previous experiences. Instead, find out as much as you can about your predecessor's approach to the job. Focus on facts, avoid assumptions and remember that your knowledge will still be incomplete. Establish, if you can:

- why your predecessor left
- what sort of management style he or she had and how this differs from your own
- what needs to be changed in the job and when – are there urgent issues to address?

Form tentative plans in advance about what you aim to do in the job and what you want to achieve, as it is difficult to plan once you start work. But don't depart too much from established practice, at first.

3 Make the most of your induction

On your first day you should be met by someone from HR, or perhaps your line manager, who will show you around, introduce you to other colleagues, attend to formalities and introduce you to your team. Be proactive during your induction; for example, ask about anything you want to know that has not been covered.

4 Develop yourself to match the demands of your new role

Reflect on your strengths and weaknesses and consider which skills and roles you need to develop. Use your positive characteristics to advantage and to compensate for your less strong points. Consider taking a management qualification.

5 Get to know your team

Getting to know your team is an immediate priority. Focus on understanding the purpose of your department, team or unit. What is the state of play? What work is taking place? What are the expectations of your customers?

Gather your new team together if possible, even if they are in dispersed locations. Introduce yourself, tell them you are looking forward to working with them, discuss their current work and team objectives, and say that you will meet them all individually as quickly as possible. When you do see individuals, be generous with your time. Plan a framework for discussion, and take a friendly but businesslike approach. Be courteous, listen carefully, and focus on and seek information about each person as an individual. If you take any notes, explain why you are doing so.

6 Get to know your manager

Let your relationship with your manager develop gradually. Get a feel for how to time your approaches, and find out how closely he or she wants to work with you. Consider what needs to be covered in your first discussions, and use the early days to establish goals, objectives and priorities. Ensure you get enough time with your manager to enable you to develop in your post. It may be possible, for example, to get involved in a project that involves working closely with your manager. Try to spend some time getting to know your boss better, in a relaxed atmosphere, and listen attentively for any lessons or insights.

7 Develop relationships inside and outside your organisation

Introduce yourself to your internal and external customers, to suppliers and to those who make up the network in which you will be operating. Start to build up relationships with your colleagues (especially those whose support you will need) and your customers.

8 Identify the criteria against which you will be judged

Observe and listen as much as possible to increase your understanding of your new environment. What is happening within it? Can you pick up any underlying issues? Take note of what kind of behaviour is regarded as acceptable and what is not, and evaluate what people may expect from you. Consider the performance criteria by which your boss, your peers and your internal or external customers will judge you, and how you can match those criteria. Think about who might be able to help you and what they might expect in return.

9 Work on your relationship with individuals

From the beginning, try to assist individuals to realise their full potential. Notice and show appreciation when people put in extra time and effort. Recognise people's strengths and foster their self-confidence. Be careful to fulfil any promises you make. Follow the guidance provided in the CMI Code of Practice for Professional Managers (you can find this at www.managers.org. uk/code) and resolve to:

- listen to what people are saying
- help people to understand how their jobs contribute to team effectiveness
- establish clear goals and have regular discussions on individual performance
- discuss performance honestly and set agreed actions
- help people to develop plans to improve their performance
- ensure everyone understands their specific duties and responsibilities
- provide training, development and guidance to improve performance.

Make sure that you find out about and keep in mind any established performance management or appraisal processes which aim to align personal and organisational goals and objectives, identify development needs and provide appropriate training and development.

10 Set out to develop a winning team

Research suggests that good people management skills are closely linked to the achievement of good team results, so engage with and empower team members. Try to establish group goals as quickly as you can, and involve people in setting objectives and standards, deciding priorities and setting deadlines. Set a good example by demonstrating your commitment to achieving team goals and making clear your own high personal standards through your conversation, appearance and general conduct. Be friendly and warm, not distant or aloof.

11 Take stock regularly

Review progress at the end of your first week, identifying anything that requires your time and attention. If you have made mistakes, don't beat yourself up about them: good managers learn from mistakes; bad managers repeat them. Draw up a plan for the following week and repeat this process weekly. Continue to listen and learn, and remember that the pattern of behaviour set in the first months will be hard to change later.

As a manager you should avoid:

- making unnecessary promises that could be difficult to keep
- over-managing through being too anxious to do things well
- making alliances based on first impressions.

Kenneth Blanchard
The one-minute manager

Introduction

The One Minute Manager was first published in 1982. Lambasted as trite and shallow by academics, it has since sold over 7 million copies, been translated into over 25 languages and is frequently found on managers' bookshelves. It launched a new genre of management publishing, providing the model for a host of imitations.

Background

Kenneth Blanchard graduated from Cornell University in government and philosophy and went on to complete his PhD in administration and management. In the early 1980s he was Professor of Leadership and Organizational Behaviour at the University of Massachusetts, Amherst. He wrote and researched extensively in the fields of leadership, motivation and the management of change. His book *Management of Organizational Behavior: Utilizing Human Resources* (co-authored with Paul Hersey and Dewey Johnson) is now in its seventh edition and has become a classic text.

Blanchard and Spencer Johnson, co-authors of *The One Minute Manager* (*OMM*), describe the book as an allegory, a simple compilation of what 'many wise people have taught us and what we have learned ourselves' (Introduction to *OMM*).

One-minute management

The setting of one-minute management is a young, aspiring manager in search of that holy grail, an effective manager, on whom the young man may model his thinking and actions. The aspirant manager – a cross between Le Petit Prince and Candide – is caught between the two extremes of the scientific and human relations schools: some managers get good results (but at a price that few colleagues and subordinates seem willing to support), while other managers (whose people really like them) have results which leave much to be desired.

Our hero quickly comes across a manager who gets excellent results, apparently with little effort on his part – the one-minute manager. The *OMM* has three simple secrets that bring about increases in productivity, profits and satisfaction: one-minute goal-setting, one-minute praising and one-minute reprimanding.

One-minute goal-setting

Although staff cannot know how well they are doing without clear goals, claims the *OMM*, many are not clear on priorities, and many are spoken to only when they make a mistake. The *OMM* requires managers to make clear what people are asked to do and what their expected behaviour or performance is, and to get staff to write down their most important goals on a single sheet of paper for continued clarification.

One-minute praising

This is the key to improved performance and increased productivity. Instead of catching people out for doing something wrong, the opposite is recommended: 'The key to developing people is to catch them doing something right.' There are three steps in one-minute praising:

1 Praise someone as close in time to the good behaviour as possible. If you can't find someone to praise everyday, then you should wonder why.

2 Be specific. Make it clear what it was that was performed well.

3 Share feelings – tell them how you feel about what they did, not what you think about what they did.

One-minute reprimanding

This is the key to changing the attitude of the poor performer, and there are four aspects:

1 Immediacy – when a reprimand is necessary, it is best to do it as closely as possible to the poor performance that led to it.

2 Be specific – don't tell people about your reactions or give vent to your feelings, tell them what they did wrong. Admonish the action, not the person.

3 Share feelings – once you have established what was wrong, share your feelings.

4 Tell them how good they are – if you finish on negative feedback, they will reflect on your style of behaviour, not on their own performance.

The development of one-minute management

Putting the One Minute Manager to Work was a follow-up in 1984 by Blanchard and co-author Richard Lorber (an expert in performance improvement) to flesh out some of the basic ideas that had met initial success in *The One Minute Manager*. Subtitled 'How to Turn the Three Secrets Into Skills', the 1984 book focuses on the 'ABCs' of management, 'effective reprimanding' and the 'PRICE' system.

The ABCs

- Activators – those things that a manager has to do before anyone else can be expected to achieve anything, such as goal-setting, laying down areas of accountability, issuing instructions and setting performance standards.

- Behaviour (or performance) – what a person says or does, such as filing, writing, selling, ordering, buying, etc.

- Consequence – what a manager does after performance, such as sharing feelings, praising, reprimanding, supporting, etc.

Effective reprimanding

As a consequence of performance, a manager has to distinguish between when an employee can't do something, which implies a need for training and signals a return to the activator of goal-setting, and when an employee won't do something, which implies an attitude problem and a case for reprimanding. Reprimands do not teach skills, they can only change attitudes. Positive consequences, in contrast, can influence future performance to the good, so it is important to end a reprimand with praise. This has the effect of making the employee think about their own behaviour and not that of the reprimander.

The PRICE system

PRICE takes the three basic secrets of one-minute management and turns them into five steps:

1 Pinpointing – defining key performance areas in measurable terms, part of one-minute goal-setting

2 Recording – gathering data to measure actual performance and keep track of progress

3 Involving – sharing the information recorded with whomsoever is responsible

4 Coaching – providing constructive feedback on improving performance

5 Evaluating – part of coaching, also part of reprimanding or praising.

Leadership and the One Minute Manager stresses that there is no single best method of leadership. There are in fact four styles: directing, delegating, coaching and support. Whichever style is employed depends on the situation to be managed. 'Situational leadership is not something you do to people, but something you do with people.' Blanchard turns conventional leadership thinking on its head, using the analogy of turning the organisational pyramid upside down; instead of staff working for their boss, the boss should work for the staff.

The One Minute Manager Builds High-Performing Teams can be seen as a companion to *Leadership and the One Minute Manager*. It concentrates on integrating the simplicity of the one-minute techniques into understanding group dynamics and adjusting leadership style to meet developing circumstances.

The One Minute Manager Meets the Monkey deals with the problems of time management and overload. Paying tribute to his co-author, Bill Oncken, who created the monkey analogy, Blanchard points the finger at the manager as the 'hero with all the answers' by stressing that bosses are not there to try to tackle every problem themselves, but rather to get others to come up with solutions. The monkey is the problem – or the next move – being passed from subordinate to superior, making the superior rapidly ineffective; the one-minute manager is not a collector of monkeys, but rather a facilitator and coach helping others to solve their own problems.

In perspective

Blanchard continues to write, train and consult, and an overview of his offerings can be found at www.blanchardtraining.com/. Like other well-known management writers, however, he has adopted a broader remit than the focused concepts that brought him to the attention of managers. Since the mid-1990s, he has independently or collaboratively published titles on high-performance teams, empowerment, world-class organisations, positive relationships and the power of vision. Cleverly – in that titles sell – he has included the 'time' element in the subtitles of most of these books, though with the qualification that team building and constructing world-class organisations do take more than a couple of minutes to achieve.

So where does Blanchard sit in the hall of fame of management thinkers?

At the end of the 1990s, much of the material in the *One Minute Manager* series no longer seemed earth-shattering. Countless publications and infinitely more seminars on leadership, change, delegation and time management had rendered a glance back to Blanchard unsurprising, entertaining and even comforting in its confirmation, but – like the key message from a contemporaneous publication, *In Search of Excellence* (Thomas J. Peters and Robert H. Waterman, 1982) – no longer the inspiration it was.

When asked why *In Search of Excellence* did so well, critics and commentators argued that its timing was impeccable, being published at a time when Western business concepts were being rubbished in favour of analyses of the Japanese business boom. If Peters and Waterman's book was largely about reinvigorating pride in successful American organisations, Blanchard's was excellently timed for its impact on individual skills and techniques.

It is important to remember that before Peters, Blanchard and the host of others following in their wake, management – as far as the hard-nosed manager was concerned – was a stuffy, dry subject reserved for lengthy academic treatises and exposés. Most books – and there were not many – focused on building the arguments of the human relations school and tackling the enormity of the scientific/bureaucratic establishment constructed so convincingly by Frederick Winslow Taylor, Henry Ford and Max Weber. Books on management were not popular, not widely read and certainly not bestsellers. It is often claimed that Peters and Waterman changed all that. But Blanchard's contribution was also hugely influential. *The One Minute Manager* may have been panned by academics, but it did more to make management digestible, readable and accessible to a wide audience than any of its predecessors. In the form of allegory, anecdotes and allusions, it brought management to a level where many could believe they could do it and do it well. Others have followed in the storytelling mould of *OMM*, two of which are *One Page Management* (Riaz Khadem and Robert Lorber) and *Zapp! the Lightning of Empowerment* (William Byham and Jeff Cox).

So what is the appeal of *The One Minute Manager*, rejected (like Abraham Maslow) by academia, but wholeheartedly adopted (as was Maslow) by practising managers around the world? Blanchard's book was, first and foremost, short and to the point. Moreover, it was written in readable, everyday language, offering practical, everyday solutions to practical, everyday problems. This was no dry, stuffy theory, but a collection of honest sensible techniques to try out straightaway. This is where Blanchard scored a first.

Any author that sells over 7 million copies of a book deserves a place in the management hall of fame. For Blanchard, that place has to be broadly in the human relations school alongside the great popularisers of empowerment and the self-help school, stretching from Dale Carnegie and Samuel Smiles to Stephen Covey and, lately, Tom Peters.

Blanchard's message may not be original – few messages are – but few have spread simple messages more effectively, or to such a wide audience.

Newly promoted into a managerial post

A new manager is somebody who has taken on his or her first management or supervisory position.

This checklist offers advice for first-time managers who have been promoted to a managerial role within their organisation. A promotional opportunity may have arisen as a result of organisational restructuring, or when an existing member of staff has left the role. It may be something to which you have been aspiring for some time; or it may be an unanticipated or even unwelcome surprise. Whatever the circumstances, a promotion suggests that your skills, knowledge and ability to take on a more challenging post have been recognised by senior management.

Taking up your first management role can be both an exhilarating and a demanding time. An elevation in position brings with it increased authority and control as well as increased accountability – for both your performance and that of others. As a result, the relationships you previously had with colleagues and peers may well change, with a shift in their perception of you and your view of them. To assist with your promotion to a higher grade, a selection of common situations that newly promoted managers may encounter is presented, offering advice on how to deal with each effectively. The following pointers are also worth bearing in mind:

- learn from watching and listening to your team
- reach agreement with your new manager on your responsibilities and goals

- work at developing relationships with your new manager and peers

- seek help and advice where necessary, from either your manager or the HR department

- use work-based activities and meetings as an opportunity to 'bond' with your team

- take stock regularly, learning from what went well and what did not.

Action checklist

Situation 1

After the initial celebrations, you realise that your team seem to be shutting you out – conversations dry up when you enter the room. They may go off to lunch or to the pub without you; somehow you no longer seem to hear any gossip. There may even be snide comments.

Response

This is normal. Accept that things have changed: before you were a colleague; now you are the manager. It does not mean that you cannot have friendly relationships with the people in your team, but they will, and should, be different. You have new responsibilities that will be difficult to fulfil if you do not distance yourself a little from your team. These include such things as maintaining performance levels, managing poor performance, carrying out performance appraisal discussions, handling disciplinary or grievance issues and maintaining confidentiality about sensitive issues like prospective restructuring. This does not mean that you should go to the other extreme and exert your status and authority unnecessarily or inappropriately. You are seeking the middle ground.

The initial, probably slightly extreme, emotional reactions will naturally die away after a period, provided you maintain a friendly attitude. Put a smile on your face, chat casually when it is appropriate to do so, bring in some doughnuts or suggest a drink in the pub if somebody has something to celebrate. You could, for example, get a list of your team members' birthdays from HR.

Consolidate your new relationships by bringing your team together for work-based activities. Short, regular team meetings (half an hour to an hour a week, or maybe a daily ten minutes over a cup of tea or coffee) will enable you to:

- keep track of what each person is doing and get advance warning of potential bottlenecks or crises
- share any company or departmental information you have
- get ideas to improve working practices
- deliver short, focused training on new processes and systems.

Develop relationships with your new manager and colleagues. You probably feel like the new kid on the block, but most people will remember how they felt in your position and will make you welcome. Again, smile, be prepared to make the first move, but don't be too pushy. Don't hesitate to ask for help or advice, as almost everyone will feel well disposed towards people who recognise their superior knowledge and experience.

Situation 2

Everything seemed to be going well, but now, for no real reason, your team's performance seems to have gone downhill – you have no idea what you have done wrong, but you are sure you will get the blame.

Response

Don't panic! This can be a common – and hopefully short-lived – response to the change in the team dynamics. Typically, people faced with change (and a new manager can be a major change) respond in a similar way. Initially, there may be disbelief or even denial if the change is unpleasant; then comes a period of fairly high energy and activity when work performance may be high; this is commonly followed by a period of confusion, apathy or depression leading to lack of energy and poorer work

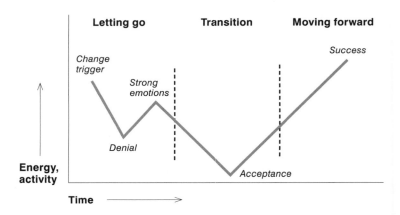

Figure 1: Typical emotional response patterns following major change

performance. This process seems to be a necessary precursor for full acceptance of the changed situation and future success (see Figure 1).

Day-to-day progress through this pattern is rarely smooth and people may often see-saw backwards and forwards.

To help your team through the change process:

- accept that they may feel regret at losing their previous manager ('At least we knew where we were with X, you could rely on him to…'); they may also feel insecure, especially if your promotion was part of a wider restructuring. Accept a certain amount of moaning and negativity, which is natural

- involve them in setting departmental goals

- show your confidence in your people and the organisation by publicly acknowledging successes

- avoid introducing more changes, if you can, until the current change has been worked through

- inform the team of any future changes, to help them to prepare for these.

Even though your promotion may be welcome, don't be surprised if your own emotions and reactions follow the same roller-coaster pattern.

Situation 3

Now you have been promoted, there are a number of things in the department that you would like to change: systems and procedures, and even the office layout. Beware! Remember the model (Figure 1) and tread softly at first.

Response

Be especially sensitive to changes in office or workplace layout. People can become attached to their particular corner of the room or desk. One of the best ways of helping a new team to work productively together is to locate them in the same working area. This is something you may want to think about if your team is currently scattered in different locations. If possible, try to base yourself with your team. Depending on the organisational culture, you may have a separate office. If so, spend as much time with them as you can. If you and your team are in an open-plan area, try to ensure that there is a private room nearby for one-to-one meetings.

Involve team members in any changes that you would like to propose. They will have their own views and may be closer to the reality of how things actually happen than you are. If appropriate, be prepared to abandon your ideas after consulting with your team. This will not be perceived as weakness, rather as you demonstrating confidence in them.

Situation 4

You don't know how to fill your day. In the past, you knew what your job was and you got on and did it – well. Now there do not seem to be many fixed tasks that you need to do, but you have an uncomfortable feeling that you are missing something and that it will rebound on you.

Alternatively, you seem to have become everybody's dogsbody. Your management job seems to consist of paperwork chores that anybody could do and dealing with all the stuff that nobody else wants to handle. Consequently, you are run off your feet but never really seem to accomplish anything.

Response

These situations are more likely to arise where the position to which you have been promoted is a new one rather than replacing a previous manager. Although the two scenarios may seem very different, they can be handled in the same way.

Establish what your manager is expecting from you and agree a job description (write your own draft if one does not already exist). As a manager you are likely to be measured according to your achievements in the following areas:

- delivery of product or service targets
- cost control
- customer satisfaction
- people management
- process, system, equipment maintenance
- future planning.

Aim to have one or two goals or performance standards in each of these areas.

Try to agree priorities with your manager, and sort out how and with what frequency your manager would like you to report on your activities and those of your team. In the early days, even if it is not a requirement, it can be useful for you to prepare a brief weekly report summarising achievements and activities. Try also to set up regular meetings with your manager. These have obvious communication benefits and will help you both to develop your relationship.

You may want to set up similar regular meetings with your direct reports. This will help you keep track of what is happening without constantly breathing down their necks, and may enable you to delegate some of those chores. Be careful that you delegate the appropriate authority as well as the tasks, or you may be perceived as just dumping the drudgery and retaining the rewards.

In many ways, as it is your team who achieve the results, your main function is to enable them to do so. It can be worth turning the organisation chart upside down.

Situation 5

Your friend John has never been the best of workers. He has always believed in doing the least he can get away with while still getting paid, and you have often covered for him in the past. Now you are his manager and responsible for the results.

Response

This can be an awkward and difficult situation. You may feel sad that your friendship with John could be affected; you may feel angry, even a sense of betrayal that John, your friend, is letting you down like this; you may feel anxious that his performance will reflect on yours; you may feel nervous that you will, at some stage, have to take formal action against him. On top of this, he may be genuinely delighted at your promotion and even expect you to go on covering for him.

You need to talk openly and informally with John as soon as possible. Explain your position to him and acknowledge that you would very much like your friendship to continue. But don't deceive yourself. The change in your position is likely to have an impact on your relationship.

If poor performance continues, do not ignore it. Try the informal approach first, probably more than once, but be prepared to take action if you need to. Be careful to treat John neither more leniently nor more strictly because he is a friend. Document any meetings.

Seek the advice of your HR representative or another manager to ensure that your perspective is not being distorted by your friendship.

Situation 6

When you first joined the department, Susan was your mentor. She had the most experience and everybody looked up to her. Susan showed you, and all the other new employees, the ropes. Admittedly, after some time you realised there were some parts of the job (mainly to do with new processes and technology) that Susan had ignored or been scornful about. You suspect that this is why you, despite your comparative inexperience, have been promoted, rather than Susan.

Response

Don't assume that Susan would have wanted the promotion and is therefore jealous and angry with you. This may be the case, but she may equally be delighted that one of her protégés has been successful.

Susan's experience and expertise will be valuable to you and the team. Tell her so, and make it clear how much you appreciated her help in the past. Involve her in areas where her strengths are useful, for instance in continuing to mentor more junior staff. However, you may want to supplement this with other support for them in new process and technology areas. If she is keen to develop further, give her special support (maybe formal training) in these areas. Make sure that your manager and other team members know that Susan is valued.

Delegate more challenging responsibilities to her as appropriate, and ensure that she receives the recognition and visibility for these achievements. If she is then promoted, be delighted in her success. At the same time, make sure you have somebody suitably positioned as her successor, should the need arise.

As a manager you should avoid:

- making promises that you may not be able to keep
- rushing into making changes
- taking up fixed positions which leave you no room to change your mind or manoeuvre.

Handling the politics

Organisational politics consists of the behaviour and personal interactions that result from the competing desires of individuals and groups to gain power and influence within an organisation. It operates through the informal rather than the formal organisational networks and systems.

Office politics is a fact of everyday working life. It arises from the desires of individuals and groups to shape organisational agendas and to enhance their own position and influence within the organisation. Organisational politics manifests itself in the context of daily workplace interactions. It carries many negative connotations: opposing groups and individuals jockeying for position; the ruthless pursuit of personal agendas; unscrupulous and unethical behaviour; infighting and back-stabbing. Political behaviour can indeed give rise to destructive conflicts, which can paralyse an organisation, render it ineffective, or damage its reputation. It can also lead to a climate of division and anxiety, which will hinder the organisation from achieving its objectives.

Politics is one of the ingredients of every organisation's informal and unofficial shadow side that runs parallel to its rational and official face. Sometimes positive and sometimes negative, the shadow side embodies natural human behaviour and cannot be ignored or swept away. Even office politics has a positive side. The complex network of personal interaction in the workplace can be a constructive force that enhances performance and enables an organisation to achieve its goals, as individuals and groups compete for recognition, preference and the lion's share of limited resources.

Ignoring the politics is not an option for those who want to achieve personal success and make a contribution to their organisation. Even if politics sometimes becomes distasteful, the best option is to try to master it and use this system ethically and with good intentions. Being aware of the complex informal networks, systems and processes that frequently contradict or overrule formal policies and hierarchies will help you to participate effectively and develop your ability to influence others. Learning to assess people and relationships, read situations and understand political nuances will enable you to manage circumstances to your advantage and that of the organisation. It can also help you to anticipate and avoid obstacles to the achievement of your personal and organisational goals. This checklist aims to give some pointers to help you develop the skills needed to navigate the political minefields of organisational life.

Action checklist

1 Consider your personal profile

An element of self-analysis is necessary when considering how you want to portray yourself to others. For example, if you want to be viewed as a trustworthy person, you will need to demonstrate honesty, openness and discretion. Be clear about how you want to present yourself and work hard to strengthen the qualities that will convey your message. Target any weaknesses you are aware of to ensure that you present yourself in the best light possible. Don't underplay your abilities or adopt an excessively humble stance, but don't exaggerate either. It will soon become evident to others if you are setting yourself up to be something you are not. Avoid behaviour which appears contrived or false and act naturally and consistently.

2 Get noticed for the right reasons

As well as your character, your appearance also says a lot about you and contributes greatly to your personal profile. Expectations regarding dress and appearance vary, so you will need to take account of cultural norms in your working environment. Consider also what your workspace says about you. Make sure you get noticed for the right reasons and remember the importance of first impressions.

3 Establish good working relationships

Your relationships with others are perhaps the most important aspect of your position in the organisation. These will inevitably affect your standing and your ability to exercise influence. Take a positive approach towards your colleagues, look for the best in them and, as far as you can, seek to be on good terms with others. Look out for people you can trust and those to whom you can go for advice and support. Take any opportunities that arise to develop relationships beyond your own department or team, as this will extend your knowledge of what is happening and raise your profile across the organisation.

4 Manage others effectively

Don't neglect your relationships with those in your immediate team, however. To some degree, the success of your team and how well they perform will determine your own success. Managing a team of people also provides opportunities for you to significantly enhance your own performance. Endeavour to make allies of your staff and remember that the way you manage your people will be observed by others within the organisation, and that they will judge you according to what they see and hear.

5 Be a good communicator

What and how you communicate are crucial to your political standing. Be articulate and consider how you can communicate clearly so that there are no misunderstandings. Get your message across in a concise and powerful way. Think before you speak. Unconsidered outbursts can be extremely destructive. Be truthful at all times. Communicate successes and achievements as a morale booster. However, remember that no one responds kindly to boasting or conversations that revolve entirely around you. Adapt your communications to different situations, tailoring them to the audience you are addressing. Refrain from exaggerating or being vague, and avoid jargon unless you are sure your audience will understand what you mean.

Body language, facial expressions and eye contact all enhance communication in ways which may be lost in written messages. When sending email messages, be especially clear in your communication, as the absence of visual clues can cause familiarity to be misinterpreted as disrespect, or irony as sarcasm. Make a judgement as to the most appropriate method of communication, both for your audience and for the message you need to put across

6 Be aware of formal and informal power networks

Every organisation has informal sources of power and authority as well as formal organisational structures and reporting lines, official policies and procedures. The latter are easier to grasp as they are set out in organisation charts and documents; the former are unwritten and often unspoken. Observe how people behave, practise your listening skills, ask incisive questions and look out for examples of politically motivated behaviour. Take note of the tactics being employed, try to assess the unwritten rules of behaviour in the organisation and to discover how things work and who are the key influencers and shapers.

7 Establish a personal network

Use the opportunities you have for networking to identify and develop relationships with people who are willing to assist and support you in your development. Your network of contacts will consist of different people from across the organisation. Each will bring different elements to the relationship. Seeking out contacts to fulfil some, or all, of these functions will significantly enhance your chances of success:

- **Sources of information** – those who are in the know and are willing to share their knowledge.

- **Gatekeepers** – those who are not necessarily important in their own right but have the power to allow or deny you access to the key players.

- **Influencers** – those who are able and willing to help you develop and, more importantly, have the seniority to make things happen.
- **Mentors** – those who provide advice, support and encouragement.
- **Developers** – those who actively help you to learn.
- **Stimulators** – those whose engagement acts as a catalyst for your own ideas.
- **Role models** – those whose example you can learn from.
- **Soul mates** – those whose friendship keeps you grounded and on course.
- **Swappers** – those with skills complementary to your own with whom you can 'swap' skills.
- **Promising talents or protégés** – those less senior than you who can nevertheless help by introducing fresh new ideas.
- **Your team** – those reporting to you who can help to raise your profile as a good manager.
- **Devil's advocates** – those prepared to offer constructive feedback.

Keep an eye on the changing dynamics of relationships within your network and be aware of the need to maintain and manage your relationships. Keep track of changing roles, responsibilities and positions and be prepared to add to your network of contacts when necessary. As far as possible, be someone who will give or return a favour when called upon to do so.

8 Take advantage of meetings

Meetings give you an opportunity to influence decisions, enhance your image and develop your political standing. You can make a good impression by doing basic things such as being punctual. Make sure that you read any pre-circulated documents, as this will enable you to make a useful contribution. Take an active part, but avoid dominating the discussion. Provide reasoned arguments while maintaining a calm exterior, and communicate with authority and confidence as you put your point across. Make yourself known to those present – they could become useful contacts further down the line.

Be on the alert for 'hidden agendas' at meetings. You may find that delegates have their own ideas about what should be achieved and may have conferred with others before the meeting to get their support. A 'successful' meeting will mean very different things to those present. Watch out for strategies such as exaggeration and needless delaying tactics.

9 Use informal communication channels with care

The office grapevine can be a useful means of obtaining unofficial information. However, be aware of spreading rumours and gossip – you may find yourself the subject of negative feedback. Using the grapevine effectively depends on involving the right people. It can be used to put a message 'out there' quickly if it is given to the 'right' ear. Take care, though, as your message could easily be distorted or misunderstood as it passes from one person to another.

10 Spot the pitfalls

Watch out for potential pitfalls when seeking to exercise influence. Some people may want to progress at your expense and will be only too happy to trip you up if you give them the opportunity. Be aware of your allies and your adversaries, and watch out for those who appear to be friends but in fact have a hidden agenda of their own. If you perceive someone as being 'neutral', don't automatically assume that they will be on your side. Learn to read between the lines and don't take everything people say at face value. Be prudent and vigilant and not too trusting until you get to know someone well. Listen to what is being said, and how it is being said. Use your own judgement and always trust your instincts.

11 Plan ahead

To manage the politics surrounding you, you will need to have clear aims in mind as to where you want to be and what you want to achieve. Define your objectives and have clear long-term goals. Think about where you are now; where you want to be; how you'll get there; and where to go once you've reached your destination. Think about your choice of contacts and what you need from them in order to achieve your objectives. Take advantage of opportunities as they present themselves and avoid anything destructive that will throw you off course. Take a long-term view and avoid jumping at a short-term advantage that may turn out to be a dead end. Constantly monitor your environment and those around you as things can change quickly. To be successful in office politics, you need to react and respond to change.

12 Don't engage in underhand tactics

Do all you can to be authentic and maintain your integrity. There may be times when you need to be assertive if you are to get what you want. A degree of ruthlessness may be called for on occasion, but use this in moderation and don't be underhand or antagonistic towards your adversaries. Remember, how you behave will be observed by others. If you engage in underhand tactics to 'trip up' an adversary, you are laying yourself open to similar treatment from others; this could damage your reputation and threaten your career progression at the same time.

As a manager you should avoid:

- sticking to the same network of people as your career progresses
- focusing purely on short-term goals
- being overly trusting and taking everyone at face value
- choosing the wrong mode of communication to convey your message
- underestimating the importance of first impressions
- being devious and underhand.

Testing for personal effectiveness

Personal effectiveness is the ability to perform specific, functional tasks and includes personal qualities, aptitudes and attitudes. Personal skills may also be called transferable skills, personal competences or personal behaviours.

A simple approach to help you to assess your personal effectiveness and identify areas for development is offered here. This checklist is in the form of a simple test, which allows you to assess your personal skills across a wide range of tasks and activities, including teamwork, presentations, stress management, influencing others, planning, relating to others and prioritising objectives. It should take no more than half an hour to complete.

The test summarises a personal competency framework designed by the European Management Association (formerly CECIOS, the European Management Council) for use in profiling managers' personal skills. It was published in *Practical Self-Development: A Step-By-Step Approach to CPD* (Institute of Management, 1997) and can be used to analyse your own skills and, if you get others to complete it for you (boss, colleagues, staff, customers, for example), as a feedback tool.

Tackling the test

1 Select relevant statements

Each of the competences in the boxes has four statements listed beneath it. Look at the statements and decide which is most relevant to your current situation at work.

2 Assess your performance

Select the appropriate statement and tick the column that best describes your own perception of your performance in that area.

3 Review the results

When you have finished the table, you will be able to review your current level of ability and performance.

4 Consider the developmental implications

The statements correspond to levels of management ranging from team leader (the first statement) to senior manager (the fourth statement). If you believe that you perform excellently at a lower level (first and second statements), you perhaps need to identify opportunities to test your skills at a higher level (third and fourth statements). Think about ways of improving areas of weaker performance.

5 Seek feedback from others

The ultimate test must be whether your colleagues, boss or reports share your assessment of your particular skill set, so it is highly desirable to compare your perceptions with those of someone who knows you well. Most managers get surprises when they do this, sometimes because they find that their worries about performance in some areas are ill founded. This is one form of '360 degree review', which is a key step in understanding your own performance.

Reviewing test outcomes

Identifying your personal effectiveness profile may be instructive, but how do you exploit this knowledge? To convert self-knowledge into action and success, you need to do four things:

1 Raise your level of awareness

Frequent and regular feedback is the only way to increase your awareness of your personal effectiveness. Look for different sources: self-assessment tools, your colleagues, your boss, your partner and friends, even customers. Find ways of asking them what they think.

2 Monitor your performance and impact

If you have key performance indicators (KPIs) that are directly attributable to your performance, these may give a strong indication of your effectiveness. Analyse these and consider what they tell you about your performance, effectiveness and strengths and areas that need development.

3 Identify your key development needs

Review the match between your current job and career aspirations and the principal aspects of your personality. Add this to what you have identified from feedback and KPIs to gain a well-rounded picture of your development needs.

4 Create realistic action plans

This is the hard part. To change your behaviour and improve performance, you need to be realistic, to set SMART (specific, measurable, achievable, realistic, timely or time-bound) objectives, to expect setbacks, to reward yourself when you succeed, and to use others to support and guide you. Most importantly, you need to review your progress on a regular basis and use feedback and KPIs to gauge and steer the impact of your actions.

As a manager you should avoid:

- being dishonest with yourself when going through the test
- taking too long to complete the test.

Personal Competence Indicator

Mark **x** in the appropriate column	Very good	Satisfactory	Needs improvement	Unsatisfactory	Not relevant
Relating to others					
Treat people even-handedly					
Actively develop team-building and interpersonal skills					
Assist other managers to develop team-building and interpersonal skills in their team					
Establish good teamwork and interpersonal skills as a key element in the corporate culture					
Teamwork					
Contribute to the development of internal teams					
Exploit the strengths and skills of staff in your area					
Develop expertise and teamwork across departments in the company					
Develop the corporate culture for promoting staff development					
Presentation					
Make effective presentations to staff and colleagues					
Make effective presentations to the senior management team					
Use professional presentations to raise the profile of the company					
Promote the company's image and mission through major public presentations					
Ethical perspective					
Comply with statutory and organisational codes of conduct					
Identify potential conflicts between the interests of stakeholders					
Identify and work towards the solution of ethical issues in the company					

Mark **x** in the appropriate column	Very good	Satisfac- tory	Needs improve- ment	Unsatis- factory	Not relevant
Create a company culture with a strong emphasis on business ethics					
Planning and prioritising objectives					
Identify objectives to meet operational requirements					
Translate business plans into operational objectives for your team					
Evaluate and integrate the plans of other managers into corporate business plans					
Create the company's mission and set the strategy					
Commitment to excellence					
Consistently seek quality results in your own performance					
Motivate your team to achieve high-quality standards					
Motivate other managers to achieve high-quality standards in key areas					
Set ambitious, realistic goals for yourself and the rest of the company					
Influencing others					
Achieve targets through staff without recourse to inappropriate confrontation					
Secure maximum contributions from staff towards achieving business plans					
Persuade other managers to change their direction and attitudes in key areas					
Gain internal and external support for the company's mission and strategy					
Information search					
Collect information to monitor operation performance					
Investigate and take advantage of all possible sources of information related to your area of responsibility					
Forecast major trends in your area of business in the company					

Mark x in the appropriate column	Very good	Satisfac- tory	Needs improve- ment	Unsatis- factory	Not relevant
Apply information about the wider business environment to make decisions on future corporate direction					

Self-confidence

Put your ideas into action					
Take action to ensure performance targets for your area are consistently exceeded					
Create new opportunities outside your normal area of responsibility					
Create a feeling of optimism and entrepreneurship within the organisation					

Managing stress

Take advantage of formal processes within the company to reduce stress					
Consult with others to reduce levels of stress within your team					
Reduce the effects of constant pressure through careful planning					
Implement unpopular or stressful plans at company level					

Personal learning and development

Use feedback to identify development opportunities for improved personal performance					
Actively seek opportunities for self-development in line with company requirements					
Demonstrate an excellent track record for career development supported by comprehensive feedback					

Strategic perspective

Develop clear plans to achieve results within the context set by others					
Reduce complex issues to practical steps and plan activities which take the endeavour forward					
Relate key activities and decisions to long-term strategic aims					

Mark x in the appropriate column	Very good	Satisfac-tory	Needs improve-ment	Unsatis-factory	Not relevant
Create and direct a clearly defined vision of the future within the company					
Analysis					
Apply a practical, accurate approach to operational problems					
Use detailed analysis to direct the future actions of your staff					
Identify new approaches to implementing plans outside your area of expertise					
Generate ideas and create effective strategic plans at corporate level					
Judgement					
Use facts to arrive at simple operational decisions					
Use adequate information to support decision-making within your area of responsibility					
Use a variety of information and tools to make decisions at a corporate level					
Make consistent decisions on behalf of the whole organisation					
Organisational influencing					
Use 'informal systems' to get things done					
Create your own plans to alter attitudes or activities within the company					
Influence major corporate decisions					
Achieve major changes in the culture and direction of the company					

Stephen R. Covey
The seven habits of highly effective people

Introduction

In *The Seven Habits of Highly Effective People*, Stephen Covey (1932–2012) offered a holistic approach to life and work that struck a significant chord with the perplexed manager working in turbulent times.

Covey was co-founder and vice-chairman of FranklinCovey, a global professional services firm. In 1985, he founded the Covey Leadership Center – now part of FranklinCovey – and the Institute for Principle Centred Leadership in Utah. Born in 1932, he gained an MBA from Harvard Business School and a doctorate from Brigham Young University, where he was subsequently Professor of Organizational Behavior and Business Management.

At the Covey Leadership Center, through his writing – chiefly *The Seven Habits of Highly Effective People* (which has sold over 5 million copies) – and consultancy (he was invited to Camp David by President Clinton), his message reached millions of individuals in business, government and education.

The recurring themes in his various works are: the transforming power of principles rooted in unchanging natural laws that govern human and organisational effectiveness; adapting every aspect of one's life to accord with these principles; effective leadership; and empowerment. Here, we will concentrate on *The Seven Habits of Highly Effective People*, while introducing his more recent idea of an eighth habit. Covey died in hospital, following a bicycle accident. He was 79.

The Seven Habits of Highly Effective People

The seven habits are addressed to readers not only as managers but also as members of a family, and as social, spiritual, sporting and thinking individuals. They offer a 'life-transforming prescription' which calls for a rethink of many fundamental assumptions and attitudes (paradigms).

The seven habits build on the fundamental concept of interdependence. Covey traces a personal development outline from dependence in childhood (many people never grow out of a dependency culture), through independence in adolescence (self-assurance, developing personality and positive mental attitude), to interdependence – recognition that the optimum outcome results from everyone giving of their best, each aiming for the common goal with shared mission and vision but freedom to use their best judgement on how to go about achieving that common goal.

Habit 1: be proactive

Covey distinguishes between proactive people – those who focus their efforts on things that they can do something about – and reactive people – those who blame, accuse, behave like victims, pick on other people's weaknesses and complain about external factors over which they have no control (such as the weather).

Proactive people are responsible for their own lives. Covey breaks down the word responsibility into ability and to choose a response. Proactive people recognise their responsibility to make things happen. Those who allow their feelings to control their actions have abdicated responsibility and empowered their feelings. When proactive people make a mistake, they not only recognise and acknowledge their mistake, but also correct it if possible and, most importantly, learn from it.

Habit 2: begin with the end in mind

Leadership is about effectiveness – the vision of what is to be accomplished. It calls for direction (in every sense of the word), purpose and sensitivity. Management, in contrast, is about efficiency – how best to accomplish the vision. It depends on control, guidance and rules.

To identify the end, and to formulate your route or strategy to achieving that end, Covey maintains the need for a principle-centred basis to all aspects of life. Most people adopt something as the basis (or pivotal point) of their life, such as spouse, family, money, church, pleasure, friends (and in a perverse way, their enemies) and sport. Of course, all these have some influence on the life of every individual. However, only by clearly establishing your own principles, in the form of a personal mission, do you have a solid foundation.

Habit 3: put first things first

Covey's first major work, *First Things First*, set out his views on time management. It is not a case of managing time, but of managing yourself, focusing on results rather than on methods in prioritising within each compartment of work and life.

He breaks down life's activities into four quadrants:

- **Quadrant 1: Urgent and important** – for example, crises, deadlines, unexpected opportunities
- **Quadrant 2: Not urgent, but important** – for example, planning, recreation, relationship building, doing, learning
- **Quadrant 3: Urgent, but not important** – for example, interruptions, meetings
- **Quadrant 4: Not urgent and not important** – for example, trivia, time wasters, gossip.

Essentially all activity of effective people should focus on the second quadrant, apart from the genuinely unpredictable quadrant 1 events. However, effective planning and doing in quadrant 2 should minimise the number of occasions in which crises occur.

The outcomes of a quadrant 2 focus include vision, perspective, balance, discipline and control. By contrast, the results of functioning within the other quadrants are:

- **Quadrant 1:** stress, burnout, inability to manage time (and thus loss of control of your own life)

- **Quadrant 3:** short-termism, loss of control, shallowness, feelings of being a victim of circumstances

- **Quadrant 4:** irresponsibility, dependency, unsuitability for employment.

Habit 3 is therefore about managing yourself effectively, by prioritising according to the principles adopted in habit 2. This approach transcends the office diary or day-planner, embracing all roles in life: as manager, mentor, administrator and strategist; as parent, spouse and member of social groups; and as an individual with needs and aspirations.

Habits 1–3 are grouped under the banner 'Private Victory'. They are about the development of personal attributes which provide the foundations for independence. Habits 4–6 are described by Covey as the 'Public Victory', as they are the basic paradigms of interdependence.

Habit 4: think win/win

Interdependence occurs when there is cooperation, not competition, in the workplace (or the home). Covey holds that competition belongs in the marketplace.

He points out that, from childhood, many people are conditioned to have a win/lose mentality by school examinations, parental approval rationed to 'success', and eternal comparisons and league tables. This results in a 'scarcity mentality', a belief that there is only a finite cake to be shared: such a mentality is evident in people who have difficulty in sharing recognition or credit, power or profit. It restricts their ability to celebrate other people's success, and even brings about a perverse satisfaction in others' misfortune.

By contrast, Covey advocates an 'abundance mentality' which:

- recognises the unlimited possibilities for positive growth and development
- celebrates success, recognising that one person's success is not achieved at the expense, or to the exclusion, of others
- understands and seeks a win/win solution.

He argues that to be true to your ideals, it is sometimes necessary to walk away, if the other party is interested only in a win/lose outcome. Covey describes this as 'win/win or no deal'.

Habit 5: seek first to understand, then to be understood

'I just can't understand my son … he won't listen to me.' The absurdity of this statement is highlighted by Covey in emphasising the importance of listening in order to understand. Clearly, parents need to stop and listen to their son if they truly want to understand him.

However, most people want to make their point first, or are so busy looking for an opportunity to butt into the conversation that they fail to hear and understand the other party. Covey defines the different levels of listening as:

- hearing but ignoring
- pretending to listen ('Yes', 'Oh', 'I see')
- selective listening (choosing to hear only what we want to hear)
- attentive listening without evaluation (such as taking notes at a lecture)
- empathic listening (with intent to understand the other party).

True empathic listening requires a great deal of personal security, as we are vulnerable to being influenced, to having our opinions changed. 'The more deeply you understand other people,' Covey said, 'the more you appreciate them, the more reverent you feel about them.'

Likewise, when we feel that someone is genuinely seeking to understand our point of view, we recognise and share their openness and willingness to negotiate and to reach a win/win situation.

Habit 6: synergise

The essence of synergy is where two parties, each with a different agenda, value one another's differences. Everything in nature is synergistic, with every creature and plant being interdependent with others.

We also have personal effectiveness where there is synergy at an individual level, where both sides of the brain are working in tandem on a problem or situation – the intuitive, creative, visual right side, and the analytical, logical verbal left side combining to achieve the optimum outcome.

Synergy is lacking in insecure people: they either clone others, or else try to stereotype them. Of such insecurity is born prejudice – racism, bigotry, nationalism and any other form of pre-judging others.

Habit 7: sharpen the saw

The seventh habit is about renewal: just as a motorcar or any other sophisticated tool needs regular care and maintenance, so too do the human body and mind.

Covey's metaphor is about a woodcutter who is labouring painfully to saw down a tree. The saw is obviously in need of sharpening, but when asked why he doesn't stop and sharpen the saw, the woodcutter replies: 'I can't stop – I'm too busy sawing down this tree.'

The warning is clear. Everyone can become so engrossed in the task in hand that the basic tools are neglected:

- 'the physical self' – which requires exercise, a sensible and balanced diet, and management of stress
- 'the social/emotional self' – which connects with others through service, empathy, synergy and which is the source of intrinsic security

- 'the spiritual self' – which through meditation, reflection, prayer and study helps to clarify and refine our own values and strengths, and our commitment to them
- 'the mental self' – building on our formal education through reading, visualising, planning, writing and maintaining a coherent programme of continuing personal development.

In 2004 Covey published a sequel to *The Seven Habits of Highly Effective People* called *The 8th Habit: From Effectiveness to Greatness*. In it he argued that today's new reality requires a sea change in thinking: a new mindset and a new skill set – in short, a whole new habit. For Covey, the crucial challenge of today's world is to find our voice and to inspire others to find theirs, engendering a higher level of empowerment throughout organisations so that people can align themselves closer to their organisations.

In perspective

Commentators have both attacked and applauded Covey's approach for mixing the self-help message which can be traced back to Samuel Smiles, the positive self-drive of winning friends and influencing people (Dale Carnegie), and current management theories and religious fervour.

In times of change and confusion, however, when failure, redundancy and unemployment dominate individual thinking and lead to stress, Covey's message offers the individual something to hang on to. *First Things First*, co-authored with Roger and Rebecca Merrill, has achieved twice the sales of *The Seven Habits of Highly Effective People* over a similar length of time.

Covey was undoubtedly a philosopher for our times, highlighting the significance of changing industrial and human relations in a post-confrontational era, and recognising the potential of the untapped resources within each individual.

Personal development planning

Personal development planning is the process of:

- establishing aims and objectives – what you want to achieve or where you want to go in the short, medium or long term in your career
- assessing current realities
- identifying needs for skills, knowledge or competence
- selecting appropriate development activities to meet those perceived needs.

Scheduling and timing are important but cannot be too regimented.

Employers are increasingly aware of the importance of investing in their staff and often put structures in place to provide opportunities for the development of employees. Nonetheless, managers also need to take personal responsibility for renewing and updating their skills and knowledge throughout their working lives. Personal development is a lifelong process of nurturing, shaping and improving skills and knowledge to ensure maximum effectiveness and employability.

Personal development does not necessarily imply upward movement; rather, it is about enabling you to improve your performance and reach your full potential at each stage of your career.

Adopting a constructive approach to personal development planning (PDP) will help you to:

- consider where you want to go and how you can get there
- revitalise technical skills that date quickly
- build up transferable skills (such as self-awareness, ability to learn, adaptability to change, empathy and good time management)
- monitor and evaluate achievements.

The process of PDP provides a schedule to work to and can lay the basis for:

- continuous learning
- a sense of achievement
- ensuring employability and survival in an age where few jobs can be guaranteed to stay the same
- making the most of opportunities which may arise.

Action checklist

PDP is usually understood as a cyclical process – there is no need to start at the beginning if you have already decided where

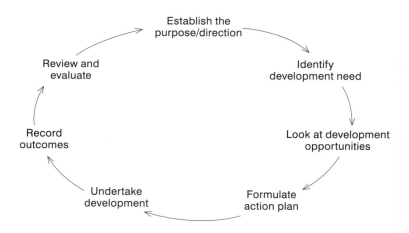

Figure 2: The personal development planning cycle

you are going and what you need to do to get there. Figure 2 outlines the process.

1 Establish your purpose or direction

The purpose of any development activity needs to be identified. You may do this either by yourself or with the help of your manager, mentor, colleagues, or friends. This involves:

- gaining an awareness of your potential within your chosen field or sector
- measuring what you are good at and knowing what you are interested in
- taking account of the organisational realities you encounter
- linking your plans to organisational needs as much as possible.

Think about:

- your own value system, involving private life and family, work and money, constraints and obstacles to mobility, now and in the future
- the characteristics of the kind of work that fits with your value system.

2 Identify development needs

The identification of development needs may emerge from intended or actual new tasks or responsibilities, from discussions with your manager or others, or from dissatisfaction with current routines. Some people know what they are good at, others may be less sure. Various instruments such as self-assessment tests, benchmarking exercises and personal diagnostics are available to help you assess your skills in a structured way.

Your development needs will depend largely upon your career goals. If you intend to remain in similar employment, you may need development to re-motivate or reorient yourself, or to improve your current performance and effectiveness. Alternatively, development may be required to prepare you for promotion, your next job, a new career or self-employment.

3 Identify learning opportunities

As a result of one or several of the assessment processes above, draw up a list of the skills or knowledge you need to acquire, update or improve. Compare this list with your current skills and knowledge and identify the gaps.

Consider:

- your learning style – some people learn best by trying out new things, while others prefer to sit back and observe; some prefer to put things to the test, others to carry out research. An instrument for identifying preferred learning styles, 'The Learning Styles Questionnaire', has been devised by Peter Honey and Alan Mumford

- your development – in addition to your own organisation, consider government and private advisory agencies, literature and open-learning aids, multimedia or online packages, professional institutes, your peer groups, networks and colleagues, and family and friends

- the range of learning options available – these can be broadly differentiated into three categories:

  - **Education** takes place over a sustained but finite period of time, usually leads to a qualification and may open up the way into a new career direction.

  - **Training** is carried out at a specific time and place and is usually vocationally relevant and limited to specific measurable aims and objectives.

  - **Development** encompasses a large number of activities with learning potential that are either work-based (such as work shadowing, job rotation, secondment, attachment, mentoring, delegation, counselling or coaching) or personal (such as private reading, authorship, presenting papers, peer-group contacts, networking, or community involvement).

4 Formulate an action plan

For each of the skills and knowledge gaps you identify, set yourself development objectives. These need to be SMART (specific, measurable, achievable, realistic and timely). There must be an element of challenge in them so that they stretch you as an individual and carry you on to new ground. But they must also be attainable and viable within a realistic time frame, otherwise time will overtake you.

5 Undertake the development

Put your plan into action – what you do and how you do it should be your choice. In addition to training courses, options include work shadowing, secondment, job rotation, project work, networking and community involvement.

6 Record the outcomes

Keeping records serves to remind you and others, such as potential employers, what you have done. Most importantly, your records will help you to focus on what you have got out of your development activity. Record the date, the development need identified, the chosen method of development, the date(s) when development was undertaken, the outcomes and any further action needed.

7 Evaluate and review

Evaluation is the crucial stage in the self-development cycle. There are two issues you should reflect upon: whether the development activity you have undertaken was appropriate and worthwhile; and whether and how your skills or working behaviour have improved as a result. Evaluating development activities also involves asking the following questions:

- What am I able to do better as a result?
- Has this experience thrown up further development needs?
- How well did this development method work?

- Could I have gained more from this activity?
- Would I follow this approach again?

  Evaluation will also provide an important lead for the next stage of the continuing cycle. Goals change, tasks vary and new needs will emerge. It is important to revise your plan accordingly.

As a manager you should avoid:

- repeatedly putting off planning your personal development
- trying to tackle everything at once – select one area to work on and then move on to the next
- being too ambitious – development normally takes place in incremental steps
- being afraid to ask for help from your line manager, colleagues or HR department
- forgetting to reflect on and evaluate your learning experiences.

Working out a career plan

Career planning is traditionally understood as the process of assessing personal strengths, values and aspirations; establishing goals and objectives; identifying the steps needed to achieve them; and putting this information into a written career plan, which will then be periodically reviewed and updated.

The importance of taking control of your career and accepting responsibility for your own career progression cannot be overestimated. Developing a career plan is part of that responsibility. Proactively managing your career can ensure that you follow a career path that will fulfil your own values, interests and ambitions and meet your professional and personal objectives.

Career management isn't a single intervention, but rather a continuing strategy. However, there are times when your career will require more input, especially if you are looking for a job move or promotion.

Regular attention to and reflection upon your career aims will help you to plan your longer-term career targets and the smaller steps involved in reaching them. A career plan gives you a useful benchmark, and allows you to develop a realistic picture of your progress. It will also increase your chances of ultimate success. Time spent on reflection is never wasted – it will help you to identify your unique mix of skills, strengths and limitations and how these may change over time. Reflection leads to clarity, so that when opportunities emerge you are able to make informed choices.

Working out a career plan will ensure that you spend time understanding and organising yourself, so as to make the most of and build upon your talents and abilities. You will then feel more confident about your future, and this confidence should be reflected in your general behaviour at work, or in interviews. Being career-conscious, having plans for the future and working on your own development all contribute to your overall employability.

Action checklist

1 Who am I?

The foundations of any plans for the future are based on your understanding of who you are, what is important to you, and your dreams and hopes for the future. This understanding helps you to begin a process of decision-making about the future.

Some simple questions can help you reflect on your career:

- What has triggered your job moves in the past?
- What are the significant influences in your life, and how have these affected your career?
- What are your skills?
- What do you see as your strengths?
- What are your limitations?
- How do others see you?
- What have been your successes and failures?
- What values underlie your life?
- What are your current obligations and commitments?
- Do you have talents that you feel are underdeveloped?
- Do you feel in a rut of any kind?
- Are your answers to the above an accurate reflection of yourself?

2 What do I want?

Once you have completed a review of where you are, you can begin to focus on the future – where you see yourself going. You should not be restricted by the normal constraints of realism at this stage.

Ask yourself: Where do I want to be in the short, medium and long term?

3 No change

At this stage, you may decide that you don't wish to make any changes to your life. It could be that you feel that your current life does not need enhancement, or, after reviewing your obligations and commitments, you may decide that this is not the right time for change and that plans for the future should be deferred. Whatever reasons lead you to opt for 'no change', the decision should be a positive and conscious one, arrived at by choice rather than default.

4 What change options do I have?

If you decide that you want to consider possibilities for change, there are many ways of approaching this. For example, you may decide to:

- make a big change in one area
- make a small change in one area
- make several small changes
- plan changes over quite a long period
- make changes as soon as possible.

5 Changing your current position

Within your current job, there may be ways to enhance what you are doing and so increase your job satisfaction. For instance, you could:

- undertake a new project

- organise a visit to another department
- participate in a job swap or consider more formal secondment possibilities
- volunteer for new responsibilities
- look for alternative ways of doing things
- offer to coach new juniors
- negotiate a redefinition of your job role to stretch you further
- shadow a colleague
- investigate the options of part-time, job share, or flexible employment.

6 Changing yourself

Changing your situation may mean changing yourself by learning new skills or updating rusty ones, setting yourself more realistic expectations or more ambitious targets, or re-examining attitudes. For instance, you could:

- attend a course or training programme
- undertake an external course of study
- encourage feedback and seek advice from someone you respect
- consult a careers adviser.

7 Changing your job

Networking is important, whether you are looking for opportunities with your current employer or externally. Make use of any internal networks as well as online networks such as LinkedIn, a business network. You will need to follow up useful contacts, or establish new ones in career areas you are attracted to. If you want to change your job completely, it is worth examining your situation positively when making career plans; think of creative solutions to ensure as close a match as possible between what you want and what is available. Consider whether, for example, you:

- can identify gaps in your skills

- have the time to update your skills or learn new ones
- can polish up your interview techniques
- need to revise your CV.

There is no guarantee that the right job will become available at the right time or that your applications will be successful. Don't limit yourself to thinking about opportunities which offer promotion; it could, for example, be time to think about a sideways move to broaden your experience, or to increase your job satisfaction.

8 Updating your plan

As time passes you may find that you have overestimated some abilities and underestimated others; or that you have discovered capacities you did not realise you had; or that circumstances have made some of your skills redundant and others more important. Your career plan will need regular revision. You should go through the review processes outlined here regularly, and certainly no less than once every three years.

You should avoid:

- having unrealistic aspirations – be sure to seek feedback on your ideas from peers, mentors, colleagues, family and friends whom you can trust to be honest

- limiting your ambitions too much – viewing yourself as able to do only one type of job will narrow your career ambitions dramatically

- over-detailed planning – this will leave little or no scope for responding to any changes in circumstances that may occur

- dependency – do not expect your present employer, or anyone else, to take care of your career plans for you

- taking unnecessary risks – your choices should always be well-informed ones.

Writing your CV

A curriculum vitae (CV) is a crucial tool for job hunting. Essentially, it is a printed or electronic document which describes you – your career history, education and personal details – painting an attractive but accurate portrait of your skills, knowledge, experience, achievements and interests.

It is important not to underestimate the significance of a CV, especially as it may be the first and only information a prospective employer receives about you. A CV is a prime marketing tool that should show prospective employers how you could meet their needs. It has been estimated that most recruiters devote only 15 seconds to reviewing a CV before making an initial decision about the candidate, so it's essential to highlight your skills and achievements in a clear and positive way. Your aim is to create an immediate interest to ensure the recruiter recommends or calls you for an interview. To do this, your CV must stand out from the many others they will have received.

When compiling or updating your CV, be sure to choose the format that works best for you and make your message simple and succinct. First impressions really do count, so make sure the layout is easy to follow and that there is enough white space to make it appear uncluttered. Be sure to sell yourself and your achievements clearly and positively, and tailor the CV to the particular position you are seeking. One CV will not necessarily fit all circumstances. Once you have put the CV together, read it from the potential employer's point of view, or at least ask a friend or colleague to offer advice.

Action checklist

1 Produce a CV that has impact and is factual and brief

Your CV should be:

- positive – more than just a list of responsibilities
- clear – written in understandable language
- neat – the best standard you can achieve in content and layout
- short – preferably two sides of A4, or the equivalent in electronic format.

It is essential that your CV is as easy to read as possible. Use headings (personal, education, experience, etc.) and bullet points.

2 Identification details

This important information forms the head of the document and consists of:

- full name
- address
- telephone numbers: home and others where you are contactable
- email address.

Organisations often remove this information before the CV is reviewed to comply with equal opportunities policies.

3 Decide on a suitable format

The two most commonly used CV formats are chronological or functional/skills-focused:

- Chronological – this is the most widely used format. As it suggests, this style of CV follows your career back in a historical manner, which works well for those who have made significant incremental moves. However, gaps on the CV will be obvious.

- Functional – this style of CV highlights the main skill areas such as management, people, operations, finance, budgets and IT. It is particularly appropriate for those who have developed their career on the basis of their transferable skills.

Your CV should be prepared in both printed and electronic formats for use in different situations. Most companies and recruitment agencies now use online as well as traditional recruitment methods, and many websites allow you to post your CV online for potential employers to see. An online CV should be formatted in a simple and clear style that looks good on-screen. Keep the page size to A4 and avoid fancy fonts, italics, underlining, colours and shading, as these may not reproduce well on computers with different screen resolutions or operating systems.

4 Preparation

Identify your key selling points, consider your career, and starting with your last job role work backwards in chronological order stating:

- job title – with clarification if necessary
- outline of responsibilities – including the number of people managed
- main achievements – the areas where you have made positive contributions or achieved identifiable outcomes.

The most detailed information should be provided about your most recent post, with detail reducing as you go back in time (unless a post was of special relevance to the one you are applying for now). Posts held more than about ten years ago should usually be listed only by responsibilities.

5 Consider including a personal statement or profile

This can give you the opportunity to present yourself as the kind of person the prospective employer is looking for. It is usually placed at the top of the CV below the identifying details and should consist of a brief paragraph – one or two sentences – to encapsulate in a nutshell who you are and what you have to offer.

Don't try to cover everything here – pick out the key points in relation to the job you are applying for.

6 Describe your achievements as your own

A CV is essentially a selling tool. By using active words, such as analysed, achieved, created, developed, designed, implemented, specialised or led, a positive picture of your skills can be developed. Use phrases such as:

- 'The systems I designed are now contributing to the success of the organisation.'
- 'I designed and successfully introduced new procedures.'

This approach is valuable for both chronological and functional formats.

7 Provide details of your education

In chronological order list:

- schools/colleges attended at secondary level and above
- qualifications obtained
- professional qualifications and memberships.

If possible, each qualification should be limited to just one line. Include details of work-based development and training if appropriate. However, if you attend short courses regularly, include only those of relevance to the post applied for.

Think carefully about where education should be placed in your CV. If you have been studying in the past five years, or if you have completed a qualification relevant to the role, place it towards the beginning.

8 Decide on further personal details you wish to include

This information may include:

- date of birth
- marital status and gender

- driving licence

- career aspirations – but only include these if they fit with the job for which you are applying

- interests and activities – but try to strike a balance between leisure activities which are so numerous and absorbing that they leave no time for work and no outside interests at all.

Note, however, that it is becoming increasingly less common to include information such as date of birth, gender or marital status to avoid any potential for discrimination. In describing your interests, avoid vague terms such as 'clubbing', 'socialising' or 'reading', and be specific. Include details of any volunteer work you do, but don't be tempted to include activities just because you think they will make a good impression. At interview you may well be asked questions about anything you mention in your CV.

It is not necessary to include:

- height, weight or state of health

- religious or political beliefs

- photographs (unless requested)

- copies of references or qualifications

- last or expected salary (unless requested).

9 Adopt the right approach for explaining experience or skill deficits

You will rarely find the elusive 'perfect job' that exactly matches your experience and skills. You may well be applying for work in which you have little experience, especially if you are a recent graduate. In these circumstances, arrange your CV to minimise any negative effects:

- adopt a functional résumé style

- focus on your relevant educational achievements and knowledge, putting this section first in the CV if it shows you in a better light than your employment experience

- accentuate skills in non-work areas that might be relevant to the post

- emphasise personal qualities such as motivation and willingness to undertake training.

10 Physical appearance

The grammar, physical appearance and content of a CV, whether paper-based or electronic, are extremely important. Poorly constructed sentences, faulty grammar, careless spelling, illogical layout, scruffy, dog-eared or tea-stained paper, or a poor-quality photocopy may tip the balance against you, all other things being equal. Emails are particularly prone to typing errors, as many people are not proficient with a keyboard or do not use a spellchecker. You should always type your CV and then:

- check and double-check your spelling

- get someone else to read your draft

- ensure the presentation is clear and easy to read

- send a printout, not a photocopy.

Some companies scan CVs onto a computer and then use a software filter to search for key words. Online CVs are likely to be searched electronically. Use current buzzwords with care. Your CV should support the notion that you fully understand what the terms mean and imply.

11 Write a covering letter or email

The content and appearance of covering letters are also important. Use the letter to show how your experience relates to the specific opportunity or organisation and summarise key elements of your CV. Do not assume that an email is more informal than a letter; pay attention to style, grammar, phrasing, spelling and layout in the same way as you would in a printed document. Some useful phrases and tips:

- In response to an advertisement

– 'I am writing in response to the above advertisement and wish to apply for the position outlined. As requested, I attach a copy of my CV for your consideration. I am seeking an appointment where my experience can be fully utilised and I would be pleased to discuss this post in more detail.'

– One successful type of letter maps the post requirements outlined in the advertisement to your skills and experience, to clearly show how you match the role. For example, you can introduce yourself in paragraph one, say what you have to offer in paragraph two and, finally, set the scene for the next step in paragraph three by saying how and when you can be contacted if the prospective employer wishes to discuss the position further.

● For speculative applications

– 'I intend to develop my career with the accent on … I would welcome a meeting with you to discuss my CV in greater depth in the context of any suitable vacancies in your organisation. A copy of my CV is attached. If you feel my experience could be applied usefully, I would be pleased to meet with you to discuss existing or potential openings.'

Tips to help you create and use cover letters:

● Send the letter to a named person. Make sure that the organisation's name is correct as well as the address, and proofread your letter for grammatical and other errors.

● Be clear about what you want. Give clear reasons why the company should consider you.

● A professional, friendly style is usually best. Avoid the hard sell.

● As with your CV, use a standard business format for your letter to enhance its appearance.

● Target your letter. You might be responding to an advertisement or following up a phone call or interview. Each of these situations requires a different approach.

You should avoid:

- lies and exaggerations
- being afraid to ask others for advice
- losing your individuality
- neglecting your CV and failing to keep it up-to-date.

How to succeed at job interviews

Interviews are formal face-to-face meetings between existing or potential employers and existing or potential employees. In some circumstances, where a face-to-face meeting is impossible, interviews may be conducted by telephone or videoconference. This checklist focuses on selection interviews which aim to assess (or partly assess) your suitability for a job whether inside or outside your current organisation.

The recruitment or selection interview represents an opportunity to present yourself to a potential employer as someone who has the skills, experience and knowledge to do the job and make a significant contribution to the organisation. Many people face interviews with trepidation, but good interview skills can help you to make a good impression and secure the job or the promotion you seek. Whatever type of interview you face, careful preparation is a crucial factor in how you perform on the day and the impression you create.

Action checklist

1 Clarify your objectives

Always think through in advance what you want from the interview: a job offer; more information on the job and the organisation; an opportunity to meet the decision-makers. If your objective is unclear, it will be obvious to the interviewers – and these people could be significant in future.

2 Do your research

Find out as much as you can about the interview, the job and the organisation. This will involve some research, especially with regard to the organisation. This is all the more important if the organisation is an international company with a different cultural background from your own. Additional preparation may be required with regard to issues such as dress style, communication and political differences.

The interview

Make sure you know:

- how to get there
- who will interview you
- what format the interview will take (group, one-to-one, tests, presentations).

The job

A careful review of any documentation you have been sent, especially copies of the job description and the person specification, if there is one, will help you to establish:

- the extent of duties and reporting relationships
- the history and background to the appointment
- the employer's expectations of the appointee
- the conditions of employment and location of work.

The organisation

Discover as much as you can about:

- history, ownership and products or services
- size, structure and location of sites
- stability, prosperity and financial strength
- reputation, strengths and weaknesses
- competitors.

3 Know yourself

You need to create the impression that you are the best candidate for the job rather than just another runner. Review your personal experience, skills, strengths and weaknesses and evaluate what makes you special, how you fit the position, and what you have to offer. Consider how you will convey these messages to the interviewer.

4 Prepare yourself for success

Fear of failure can paralyse interview candidates. Focusing on your shortcomings or possible difficulties will lead to negative feelings which may adversely affect how you present yourself. But ignoring your weaknesses can be your downfall when answering critical questions. The key is to focus on weaknesses as well as strengths and also on strategies for overcoming them. Careful preparation can help you to think positively and create a good impression. Compare these two thoughts: 'I'm just here to make up the numbers' and 'I've been chosen from a large number of other candidates'. Be aware that the interviewer or interviewers may be just as nervous as you are. Explore techniques to help you relax mentally and physically and use whichever you find most helpful before the interview begins. Think about past experiences and why they have been successful or not and how they relate to the interview. Take yourself mentally through the possible course of the interview, make extensive notes and then review them shortly before the interview.

5 Your appearance

First impressions count. An impression is made before you respond to any questions. Ensure that your appearance is professional and smart:

- appropriate clothing is essential
- finer points including hair, nails and shoes must not be forgotten
- avoid too much perfume or after-shave
- avoid extremes of colour or pattern in clothing.

6 Prepare for questioning

Think about the questions you may be asked, and prepare appropriate answers.

Questions may include:

- **Self-assessment:** What can you do for us that someone else can't? Why should we appoint you? What are your strengths and what limits you? How would you describe your personality? How do you react to pressure and deal with deadlines?

- **Work history and experience:** Tell me a little about yourself. Why are you leaving your present position? What have been your successes? What were your failures?

- **Organisation:** How much do you know about our organisation? How long would it take you to make a meaningful contribution to our organisation? What would that contribution be? What important trends do you see in our industry?

- **Job:** Why do you want to work for us? What do you find most attractive about this position? What seems least attractive to you? What do you look for in a job? How do you see your professional future?

- **Management style:** What is your management style? Are you a good manager and why? What do you think is the most difficult thing about being a manager? If I spoke to your former boss, what would he or she say were your strengths and weaknesses?

- **General interests and knowledge:** What was the last book you read, film you saw, sporting event you attended? What do you do to relax?

7 At the interview

Before the interview begins, the following steps will help you to succeed:

- arrive at your interview with sufficient time to enable you to relax a little beforehand

- when meeting the interviewer(s), smile and make good eye contact

- use good body language (sit upright and lean slightly forward) to convey your interest and alertness
- don't fidget with your hands or keep crossing and uncrossing your legs, etc.

8 Answering questions

Bear in mind that interview questions are designed to find out about you and your suitability for the post. Listen attentively and answer succinctly. Remember, too, that you are interviewing the employer at the same time as they are interviewing you. When replying to questions you should:

- keep to the point
- structure your answer so that it is logical and easily understood
- maintain good, but not excessive, eye contact
- speak out with confidence and ensure you can be heard clearly
- look prepared and have appropriate information to hand
- project interest in the organisation and job, and be interesting in your replies and questions
- be honest – admit to limitations, and don't exaggerate accomplishments.

Answer the questions in a way which demonstrates your qualities. Use statements which:

- are assertive
- begin 'I am'
- show that you are proud of your achievements.

9 Prepare your own questions

Prepare some questions of your own in advance, relating to the job or the organisation. This helps to demonstrate your interest. Your questions should not relate exclusively to money or conditions of employment.

10 Deal positively with the closing moments of the interview

Last impressions are important. Thank the interviewers for their time, reaffirm your interest in the position and state that you look forward to hearing from them in the near future.

As an interviewee you should avoid:

- arriving late
- interrupting, arguing, overreacting or getting on your soap box
- letting your nervousness spoil the impression you make
- being evasive, speaking too quickly or giving long, involved answers
- criticising third parties, or former employers
- becoming over-familiar.

Redundancy: the next day

A job is considered to be redundant if an employer:

- is ceasing to carry on the business
- is closing down the business at the site where the job is based
- is transferring the business from the site where the job is based to another location
- requires fewer employees to do the type of work
- needs fewer employees to carry out the work at a particular site.

This checklist aims to help managers to anticipate the trauma of redundancy and to face its psychological and practical problems in a positive way. It is intended for potentially redundant employees, not employers.

There was a time when redundancy was something which happened to other people. Many of us expected to remain with the same employer throughout our careers. Today, however, lifelong employment with the same organisation is less likely. By acknowledging the possibility now, if the worst does happen, you will be in a better position to cope and you will have a plan of action that can be put into effect without delay.

Action checklist

1 Recognise that you are in a state of shock

However much you may expect it, the news that you have been made redundant will leave you in a state of shock. You are likely to go through various shock-related transitional stages and to experience a range of emotions before you accept the situation fully. Expect to feel a sense of loss regarding the familiar workplaces, people and routines, the feeling of competence that went with your job, and, perhaps, any influence, power and authority you may have had.

2 Take action but don't make decisions

On the 'day after', you are likely to be in a highly emotional state, so keep yourself active rather than try to make definitive plans for the future. Try to get some exercise and fresh air, and keep yourself physically occupied. You are not in a condition to make any decisions, so leave this until later, when you will be less prone to emotional rather than rational reactions.

3 Forget 'why me?'

'Why me?' is often the first reaction of many who suffer the pain of redundancy and cannot understand why they were made redundant, rather than someone else. Recognise that your job is redundant rather than you, and that speculation about personal aspects can change nothing – but it will prevent you from taking the action needed to counter your new situation. 'Why me?' only makes sense:

- as a legal query, if relevant to the circumstances of redundancy

- at a later stage, as an exercise to help identify possible ways of presenting yourself to greater advantage.

If you do look for reasons later on, avoid comparisons with others, and try to analyse the reasons for your redundancy as objectively as possible, with the support of someone you trust and can talk to frankly. If working on the question alone, you can help yourself to be more objective by pretending to be giving advice to someone else in the same position (we are all good at advising others).

4 Don't pretend

Make no pretence about your situation to anyone. Like many people before you, you are redundant and looking for a new job. Be dignified, but don't try to pretend to the world that nothing has changed. There is no shame in redundancy. It happens to thousands of people – in a 2008 CMI survey, 38 per cent of senior executives reported that they had been made redundant at least once in their career.

5 Prepare for action: finding another job (a job in itself)

Plan your search for new work as if it were a job in itself, with regular hours and only a reasonable period for lunch. You need to be professional about it, keeping a daily record of what you have done and a diary for leads and when you need to follow them up. You may no longer be selling your former employer's products or services but you will be promoting something far more valuable – yourself. Broaden your opportunities in the jobs market by using this period after redundancy to gain new skills. Consider voluntary or part-time work.

6 Identify sources of help

List the contact details of all the people who may be able to help you. Include any outplacement services provided by your former employer.

Don't start calling contacts immediately, and when you do call avoid giving them a 'hard luck story'. Instead, wait until you are composed enough to be professional and dignified – but display reasonable humility. You need the help of others, so don't resort to arrogance to cover for your inner feelings. Have specific objectives in mind when you contact others, rather than asking individuals for 'any help at all'.

7 Locate sources of job advertisements

Use the internet or go to the library (where most of the quality press is available for free reference) and find out which newspapers and periodicals contain advertisements for the type of job in which you may be interested. Note the day on which each is published and record it in your diary. Don't forget local newspapers. You may never have read the *Townville Bugle* before, but it may contain salvation now. The internet offers many job recruitment sites and services, and if you are a member of a professional body it may offer services to assist you to identify job openings.

8 Responding to advertisements

Prepare a CV or update the one you already have. As an alternative, prepare a biographical note, which may allow you to be more selective and flexible, though don't use this as a licence to mislead potential employers.

Remember:

- covering letters should be brief and give clear, positive reasons for considering your CV
- CVs should not exceed two sides of A4 in length
- your CV is competing with others for the reader's time
- the best CVs contain positive statements rather than a mere chronology of dates and titles
- professional presentation using white space makes a document more attractive and readable.

Check with a friend – does your proposed CV show you to the best advantage? Is it free from spelling mistakes/grammatical errors?

There are professional CV writers who advertise in the national press, but ask for a sample of their work before you commission them. You may be spending money for a mass-produced 'product' which does not reflect your individuality or achievement.

9 Beware

Evaluate ideas carefully before taking action, as some that seem to make sense at the start of your job hunt may turn out to be best avoided. For example:

● firms which advertise 'access to the unadvertised job market' do not always live up to this – some may, but others may only try to sell you expensive support packages of career development counselling and skills training. Ask for introductions to people who they have helped to find a real job

● sending your CV to every head-hunter and recruitment consultant you can identify – there will be little or no return, as these firms work for organisations rather than individuals

● placing a 'job wanted' advertisement in newspapers or journals is expensive and the success rate is low.

10 Find out about rights and support

By now you may be thinking about your rights as a redundant person. Before rushing off to see a solicitor, consider alternative sources from which you may gain information or help without incurring extra costs. Try, for example:

● information and legal advisory services available through your professional body

● government-sponsored advice services

● your trade union, if you belong to one.

You could also find out if there are any job clubs in your area, as these are designed to help individuals who are unemployed to meet other professionals in the same situation. Working together gives mutual support and affirmation of talents and competences, as well as cushioning all members from the potential isolation of the job-hunting process. Online business networks such as LinkedIn can also be a source of information, support and advice.

11 Take stock of your finances

Your 'rights' will have included a financial settlement, if only at the statutory minimum level. To manage your life until you find further employment, you will need to take stock of your assets and liabilities. In doing so:

- don't overvalue your capital items

- make dramatic cost-cutting decisions after an interval, when you are in a more stable frame of mind

- don't attempt to maintain your standard of living despite the circumstances – you may be unemployed for longer than you realise

- think in terms of 'investing' rather than spending – evaluate each item of expenditure as an investment towards obtaining a new job, and do this before you invest, not after the money is spent.

12 Record and plan

Record each day's achievements and make a plan for tomorrow. You may feel that it is time to start contacting your list of potential helpers and arranging to speak to them directly. Ensure that you are in the right mood for this before you begin, and rehearse aloud what you are going to say and how you will say it. Remember that any bad impression you may make over the telephone is impossible to recall.

13 Keep fit and healthy

At the end of each day, if you have been too busy for exercise and fresh air, try to take a brisk stroll. Remember that finding a new job is your new job, for the present, and you will be able to do it more effectively if you are fit and well.

You should avoid:

- wasting nervous energy and risking the goodwill of friends by talking about unfair treatment received

- devoting precious time to the fruitless question, 'Why me?'
- putting off the hunt for a new job – the sooner this starts, the sooner you are likely to get back into work.

Dealing with redundancy

A job is redundant when the need for that job to be done in a particular location has diminished or disappeared. This can arise in situations where a business or part of a business is being closed down or transferred to another site, or where fewer people are needed to do the work. It is the job that is redundant, not the individual.

The position you are faced with when your job has been made redundant is considered here. This checklist concentrates on managing feelings and reactions, and encourages you to take a fresh look at the types of activities that you enjoy most and the career options you now have. To cope with redundancy successfully, you must seek help whenever you need it, and remember that you are not alone.

It is also important to remember that it is your job that is being made redundant, not you personally, and that you still have skills and abilities that are valuable, both within and outside the workplace. These are the key to your later success. Take advantage of outplacement counselling if it is offered, and make the most of all possible sources of support during and after your notice period. Talk to your boss or HR manager, if you can, and to family members, friends, colleagues, recruitment agencies, legal advisers, professional organisations, trade unions, and business and financial advisers. Aim to celebrate your successes and move on.

Action checklist

1 Understand the stages of change

Typically, people faced with major changes experience similar, cyclic emotions and reactions, and their responses are likely to follow a predictable pattern. Disbelief and denial are usual, followed by strong emotions, some of which may be unpleasant. It is important to express these emotions, so they are released, and you can start to feel better and more energised. Often, these feelings can culminate with a period of apathy, depression, or even despair. Day-to-day progress through this process is rarely smooth or predictable, and people may often see-saw backwards and forwards between the different stages. While going through the process may sometimes be difficult, the stages outlined do seem to be necessary milestones on the road to acceptance of the situation, and readiness to rebuild your life for future success.

Figure 3 gives an indication of the emotional stages in many people's responses to big changes in their lives, especially when such changes are considered to involve loss rather than gain or new opportunities.

To progress through these varying stages, you need to:

- **let go** – accept that your employment has ended, say goodbye and look at it with a balanced perspective, including both the good and the bad elements

- **make a transition** – sort out the practicalities of your new life, focusing on your legal entitlements and your finances and establishing a new routine and getting yourself organised. Focus too on your skills and achievements as this will help to rebuild your confidence

- **move forward** – take stock of who you are, your likes and dislikes, skills, experience, training needs, values, goals, priorities and family constraints. Start redesigning your future and considering the options open to you, such as looking for a new job, starting your own business, studying, travelling, taking a new direction or a career break, and considering retirement. Many doors may

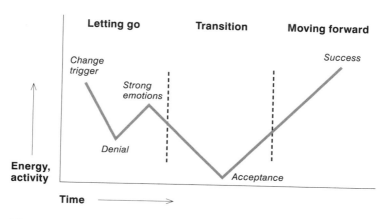

Figure 3: Typical emotional response patterns following major change

open, and you could now have the opportunity, if you wish, to break out of your current career pattern. To keep your morale high and enthusiasm strong, you may find it helpful to seek a friend or mentor, join a job seekers' support group (if there is one locally), form a group yourself (if you can't find an existing one), or employ a career consultant to help you develop your career and find the job you want.

2 Say goodbye

It is important to understand that redundancy is a form of bereavement. You have lost your employment and it is normal and reasonable to grieve. As with any bereavement, disbelief and denial are common initial reactions: 'This can't be happening to me.' 'It's a nightmare and I'll wake up soon.' 'If I keep on as usual, perhaps it will just go away.' But it has happened, and the clichés are right – time is the best healer for grief, and you need to let go of the old reality and move on to a new one. Rituals are an important part of letting go:

● list all the good times and the bad times that you recall from your time of employment – take your time over this and add to your lists whenever another memory comes into your mind

- take your list of good times and dwell on them – they are likely to centre on periods when you did things well or felt happy in your relationships with other people; in other words, they are linked to your personality and skills, and you will be able to recreate them elsewhere in the future

- take your list of bad times and look through it briefly for any lessons you may learn – then put those bad times behind you

- look again at your list of good times – remember them, enjoy them, look forward to having similar times again

- then discard both lists – they are the past

- consider developing a new list, based on things to develop for the future.

3 Learn to handle your emotions and behaviours

Although everybody's situation is different, people often experience similar emotions at this time. These can be extreme and have physical repercussions as well as affecting your behaviour. These reactions are quite normal, but seek help from your doctor if you feel that your emotions, physical reactions or behaviour are out of control.

Typical emotions include:

- anger
- anxiety
- apathy
- bitterness
- boredom
- confusion
- despair
- disbelief
- embarrassment
- guilt
- helplessness
- lack of confidence
- loneliness
- shame

Common reactions or behaviours can include:

- avoiding people
- crying
- drinking
- drug-taking
- forgetfulness
- headaches
- heart palpitations
- insomnia
- irritability
- lack of appetite
- lack of sex drive
- minor illnesses
- mood swings
- nausea
- nightmares
- over-eating
- personal neglect
- smoking
- stomach cramps
- tiredness
- violence
- vomiting

4 Organise yourself

Looking for a new job can be as much hard work as being employed. Help yourself by ensuring you have:

- somewhere dedicated to your work activities – a separate room if possible, but if not, at the very least, you need somewhere to keep your records and information

- the necessary tools for your work activities – a laptop or home computer and access to the internet and newspapers, both of which should be available via your local library

- regular working hours and a timetable of activities – one of the most disconcerting aspects of being out of a job is that your day may cease to have any markers. Give it a structure, and perhaps consider taking up some kind of voluntary activity.

List your regular tasks: scanning newspapers or internet job sites; applying for jobs; visiting or telephoning advisers; contacting your personal network; contacting companies directly; improving your skills or learning new ones. Some tasks need to be performed daily, others weekly or even less frequently. Slot them into a weekly timetable. But do allow time for relaxation. Beware of filling your timetable so much that it becomes a depressing treadmill.

Try to scatter activities that you enjoy through the week, and try to carry out at least one of these every day. The advantage of being unemployed is that you have more flexibility about when you can perform various tasks. So walk or swim in the middle of the day and send out job applications in the evening as you wish.

5 Rebuild your confidence

One of the biggest casualties of redundancy is self-confidence. To rebuild it:

- write down your past work and personal achievements – things you did that went well for you or for others, or which you felt good about, whether big or small

- identify common themes, such as your awareness of how others felt, and the skills they suggest you possess – perceptiveness, for example, or sensitivity – then add your other skills to this list

- give yourself the opportunity to use at least one of your skills every day

- identify each day's achievements and share them with family or friends – celebrate and reward yourself for your successes, however small.

6 Take stock

You will find it helpful to take stock of your life and career in various ways, and some important areas to consider are given below:

What do you enjoy most?

Enjoying work is not a pipe dream. Consider which of the following work aspects are important for you:

- using specialist expertise to work at a highly skilled level
- varied tasks and functions – no two days the same

- detailed work requiring great care and accuracy
- presenting ideas to groups of people
- seeing the 'big picture'
- selling or persuading or negotiating
- influencing or determining strategy and policy
- delivering results
- organising work
- helping other people
- working on tactical day-to-day tasks
- working with people one-to-one
- achieving work–life balance

- taking calculated risks
- working with people in meetings
- supervising other people
- working according to standard processes
- earning a lot of money
- working with IT systems
- being in a position of importance
- working closely with other people
- career progression
- working autonomously
- learning and developing skills
- training other people
- job security

What are your career options?

There are more options than just trying to find another 'permanent' job as similar as possible to the one that has ended. Look for opportunities that fit your likes and dislikes. Consider the following options:

- temporary or interim positions in your current field and industry
- working for a consultancy
- setting up as an independent consultant
- retraining for a different career

- taking a career break or sabbatical to study, travel or care for family at home
- starting your own business
- temporary, interim or permanent positions in another field or industry
- working from home

120

- voluntary work
- writing or lecturing
- retirement

- combining any of these options in a 'mix and match' portfolio

Consider constraints and priorities

Talk to family or friends about the following possibilities, listing the advantages and disadvantages of each:

- **moving house** – consider the financial implications, location, impact on children's schooling, partner's job/activities, closeness to relatives and friends, leisure interests

- **investing in a business** – consider what sort of business, where the investment stake will come from, risk versus potential profit, timing of outlay and income, legal/contractual protection, impact on family relationships

- **working from home** – consider legalities (such as your mortgage, insurance, planning regulations) and practicalities (such as a designated workspace and a working routine)

- **reducing your income** – consider whether this would be temporary or permanent, opportunities for other family members to increase their income, reducing expenditure, converting assets.

You should avoid:

- undermining your prospects by thinking 'Why me?' or seeing yourself as a victim – others will sense this

- bemoaning the situation constantly – once goodbyes have been said, move on

- becoming discouraged if the ideal opportunity does not come along immediately.

Choosing a second career

There is no commonly accepted definition of a career, but for present purposes a career is understood as the job or profession that you do for a period of your life, not necessarily with the same employer. Planning for a second career implies embarking on a course of action that will lead to a different job, profession or occupation for a significant number of years.

This checklist offers a framework within which the objectives and choices open to you in choosing a second career can be identified. It is addressed to those who see themselves presented with an opportunity to choose a second career, and those who, for a variety of reasons, feel that the pursuit or continuation of an earlier career is either impossible or undesirable.

For some, the need – or opportunity – to choose a second career has always existed. Members of the armed forces, the police and the fire services, for example, have always retired earlier than much of the population. Today, developments in the world of work – growth in the number of mergers taking place, downsizing, outsourcing and early retirement policies – have left more of us confronted with choices about how we spend the last ten or more years of our working lives.

A new career can generate fresh interests and a new lease of life; it may provide you with new friends, colleagues and associates, and opportunities to test yourself against new challenges.
However, this will depend on your temperament – do you have the energy, enthusiasm and commitment to 'start again', especially in your middle years?

Action checklist

1 Decide whether you are faced with a problem or an opportunity

Be clear about the circumstances in which you are considering a second career. For example, do you have a problem caused by redundancy or the collapse of your existing business, or a short-term problem caused by personal conflict at work? Or do you have an opportunity as a result of earlier than normal retirement (armed services, police or fire service), together with a pension that will provide you with a basic standard of living whatever the outcome of embarking on a second career? Recognise that while a problem needs a solution, the perception of that solution as a second career may be wishful thinking. Recognise also that an opportunity needs a decision and that a decision requires the assessment of relevant information and facts.

2 Decide whether you need a second career or just another employer

You may feel disillusioned with your profession and/or with the market sector in which you work. Be clear, however, that this is not a good reason for seeking to change your career, unless you are satisfied that you have some talent in other areas of activity. Ask yourself whether you are being realistic in attempting a radical change: have your interests changed, or has your balance of skills shifted, or do you feel you need a new stimulus? Talk to colleagues and friends. Satisfy yourself that you really do want a career change rather than just a new job.

3 Decide on your objectives, motives and priorities

Decide whether your aim is to achieve one or more of the following:

- enhance your income
- develop a completely new career and skills which you have not used before, either with an employer or in a self-employed capacity

- make use of your transferable skills and experience in a different sector or for the benefit of others.

4 Consider the financial issues involved in choosing a second career

These may include:

- calculating how much capital you have available for investment in a new career, should this be required

- calculating how much you need to live on and considering carefully how much you are prepared to spend, invest or lose

- considering the implications for your family, your children's education or other aspects of life which are personal and specific to your situation.

It should also be noted that in some cases a career change can be undertaken at little or no cost. It doesn't have to be expensive and it can be incorporated into an already established routine.

5 Think about training

Discover what training you will need for this second career. Find out how it can be obtained, who the providers are, how long it will take, how it may be funded and where it will take place. Remember, too, that some skills can be self-developed without 'training'. If the training is out of the area in which you live, consider whether you are prepared to be away from your family for a significant period and if they will support you in this. Remember that to move your family to the training location will take time, energy and money, and a further move may be necessary later to enable you to pursue your second career.

6 Consider status

This is a crucial point and is often overlooked. It is almost inevitable that someone moving into a new field will have to accept a reduction in status for a period, if only to establish themselves at their correct level in the new role. Those who cannot cope with this often find it more of an issue than any reduction in income. Reflect on your previous status and the power and influence you may have held and ask yourself how willingly you would forgo these. Also, ask yourself whether you would be prepared to start again at the bottom – or even the middle – of the hierarchy. Remember that you can discuss this question with whomever you choose – or with no one but yourself. You don't have to tell anyone else that you would find it difficult to handle a loss of status and prestige, but you must be prepared to recognise the fact yourself.

7 Establish what you are good at/what you wish to do

Reflect on your career so far – the achievements you have been recognised for and the skills, knowledge and experience you have gained and how these might be put to use in a new context. Try to identify what you are good at. Does your career to date show that, for example, you are good at problem solving? At your best in situations involving other people's problems? Or outstanding in crises? Compare what you are good at with what you think you might like to try. Consider vocational guidance but remember that this may cost money. Investigate additional sources of advice such as careers advisory services and ask close friends and/or colleagues what they think you are good at – it is all too easy to overestimate or underestimate your own abilities.

8 Explore the demand for what you wish to do

Make sure that there is a demand for what you wish to do and that the demand exists locally or in places to which you would – and could – happily relocate. Contact the nearest job centre to establish local levels of demand for particular skills, for example. At the same time, remember that you may not possess those skills yet.

9 Consider voluntary work

Voluntary work can provide great satisfaction and may be an attractive option if you already have a good pension. Try to identify local brokerage schemes run by organisations such as local authorities or Citizens Advice Bureaux: these will be able to put you in touch with charities which need people with skills in your area of expertise. In the UK, organisations such as REACH place skilled volunteers to provide support within a range of charitable organisations and activities. VSO seeks those able to offer help in developing countries by passing on their skills or providing organisational support, or through direct action in leading projects.

10 Talk to other people

It is important to talk to others who have taken the path that you are now considering. This includes people who have decided against seeking a second career as well as people who have chosen to embark on a new career. Try to speak to those who have succeeded, as well as to those who have failed, to get an understanding of the obstacles which could be in your path. Bear in mind, though, that individuals may have failed because of their lack of talent in the new area, rather than because their particular second career choice was a poor one in other ways.

You should avoid:

- abandoning everything in the belief that you are following a 'sure bet'

- being carried away by the glamour of new ideas rather than facing realities such as the need to make a living – does this job, profession or occupation offer you more than a reasonable chance of doing so?

- making snap decisions – consider the options and possible consequences, before taking any action.

Starting a small business

There are many definitions of a small business, but these are more relevant to business statisticians than to entrepreneurs. The Bolton Committee definition of 1971 is still one of the best: a small firm is an independent business managed by its owner or part-owner and having a small market share. For statistical purposes, the UK Department for Business, Innovation and Skills uses definitions based on the number of employees rather than turnover or balance sheet total: 0–9 micro-businesses; 10–49 small firms; 50–249 medium-sized businesses; over 250 large firms. Anyone starting a new business is considered to be involved in a small business.

Starting your own business can be exciting and rewarding. It is increasingly common for those who have been made redundant or have difficulty in finding employment to consider branching out on their own and setting up their own business – exploring a new area of interest, following a dream, or making use of the knowledge and skills they have gained in their previous employment. However, there are challenges involved and it is important to be aware of them. It's not enough just to have a good idea – you also need the right skills and temperament to make a success of the new venture. Setting up on your own involves a degree of risk, so it is helpful to know what potential problems to look out for. Many new businesses fail and one of the main reasons is poor planning, along with a lack of management skills. However, there are many sources of information and advice available to the new entrepreneur.

For many people, running their own business is simply more attractive than working for someone else, particularly since economic upheavals and uncertainty, along with mergers, acquisitions and rationalisations, have made the concept of a 'safe job' one that can no longer be relied on.

The benefits of starting your own business include:

- having control over what you do and how you do it
- achieving self-determination as your 'own boss'
- gaining independence and freedom to follow your own ideas
- enjoying the satisfaction of making a success of your own endeavours
- realising potential high financial rewards
- using your energy to promote your own interests – rather than those of others.

Challenges in starting your own business include:

- needing cash flow at the beginning
- taking risks with your own, or borrowed, capital
- working long hours
- having sole responsibility for success or failure – it rests with you alone
- being responsible for all the functions of the business – such as accounts, marketing, planning and personnel
- losing the security of paid employment – your income will be variable.

To minimise the negative impact of these challenges, it is important to make an honest and objective initial assessment of yourself. Find out as much as you can about running a business before you launch your company. For example:

- talk to people who have succeeded and those who have made mistakes

- look at what start-up help is available
- be sure to consult an accountant and lawyer before committing yourself irrevocably
- prepare a business plan in consultation with your bank.

If you carry out as much preparation and research as possible, your business will stand a better chance of succeeding despite the challenges.

Action checklist

1 Consider why you want to start your own business

If you intend to become self-employed, ask yourself:

- why you want to change your status
- if you should be seeking (alternative) paid employment
- if you have the right skills to start a business
- if you want to work long, perhaps lonely, hours
- if you can manage an uncertain cash flow
- if you have the support of your family or partner and if they understand the risks you will be taking
- if you will be able to work at and from home, if necessary
- if you have the stamina to keep going in the face of difficulties
- if friends and associates regard you as resilient
- if you have good health
- if you really do have something to offer which people will pay for – is your product or service better than others?

2 List your assets and liabilities

Your business will require capital. Whether you can afford it with or without borrowing will depend on your existing assets. What is the value of your house, life assurance policies, material possessions, shares, savings or other assets? Similarly, what is the extent of your financial commitments over the next 3–5 years? Have you considered everything? What overheads do you need to cover and what liabilities need to be accounted for? Can your assets be turned into cash? How much cash can you put on the table? Talk it over with your bank manager even at this preliminary stage. If you are considering remortgaging your house, think carefully and get as much information as possible before making a decision.

3 Ask yourself what you want to get out of your own business

You may find it beneficial to evaluate why you want to start your own business. What are you really looking for: freedom; fortune; a chance to leave the City behind; opportunities to travel, meet people or develop a fledgling idea; less responsibility? Are your motives positive – to achieve something – or negative – to get away from something? Write down your requirements and be realistic. Are you really likely to achieve them, or are you 'pipe-dreaming'? Discuss this with a friend or trusted adviser. After seeking advice and doing the necessary research, you should feel more confident and ready to proceed with your business idea.

4 Coming up with a business idea

The clearer your focus, the sooner you will be able to start detailed planning. If you don't have a clear idea, the following pointers may help:

- What existing skills and knowledge do you have which might be used in your new business?

- Be cautious about becoming 'a consultant'. Do you have the necessary expertise? Don't be misled by books purporting to tell you how to make a fortune at it.

- Find out what local opportunities there are. Monitor the local newspapers and attend events. Make the most of your existing network – opportunities can arise from the most unexpected and unusual sources.

- Identify what goods and services large companies, local authorities and other public bodies buy in from outside the area. What does the local market need?

- Research the possibility of selling goods made by others.

- Consider how you could improve on someone else's ideas, or go into partnership with them. If you try this approach alone, be aware of the provisions of patent law.

- Check changes in legislation, technology and new trends which might offer business opportunities that you may be able to take advantage of.

- Consider advertising – anonymously – your availability to invest in, and share in the management of, a small business that is undercapitalised.

5 Investigate the market for your product or service

- What is your product or service?

- What unusual goods and services are required locally?

- Who will buy your product or service?

- Why should they buy yours and not someone else's? What will be your USP (unique selling point)?

- How many people will buy your product or service?

- Is it unique or are there many like it?

- Is the market stable, growing or shrinking?

- How many competitors would you have?

- How price-sensitive are products and services like yours?

You may find it helpful to use the four Ps of marketing:

- price – is it priced to attract the right or appropriate customer base

- product – what are its benefits to customers

- place – who are those customers

- promotion – how can they be reached?

6 Decide the ideal status of the business you wish to start

Check on the types of businesses and the requirements for registration in the country where you intend to operate. Whatever your location, a number of things will need to be taken into account, such as tax and administration implications, the image of the business, legal requirements, financial issues.

In the UK there are three main types of legal status to consider when starting a business: sole trader, partnership and limited company.

You may wish to become a sole trader, operating alone, with responsibility for all aspects of the business, including taxes, debts and the day-to-day administration. If you decide to take this option, you must register with HMRC (HM Revenue and Customs) as soon as possible, otherwise you may be subject to fines. It is possible to employ other people, but ultimately the business is the individual. In this case, you are exposed to unlimited liability – if the business fails, your personal assets are at risk from creditors.

An alternative is to enter into a partnership, combining the skills and experience of two or more people. Workloads can be shared and operations can be managed more flexibly. Beware of inviting friends to join you in a proposed partnership for friendship's sake. Would they make good business partners? Do you respect their judgement? What could they add to your business?

Look for a partner whose strengths complement yours. Business relationships depend upon a balance of skills. Satisfy yourself – and your proposed partner – that you are compatible.

Establishing a limited company will restrict your liability, but you are strongly advised to consult a solicitor or an accountant before taking this step. It can be costly and complicated to set up a limited company – for example, you are legally required to maintain a minimum of £5 million employers' liability (EL) insurance. The main advantage is that the owners (shareholders) have limited liability for the debts of the business up to the value of their shareholding. The status of a limited company raises the credibility of the business in the eyes of customers and suppliers, since it suggests that it is fairly well established. Satisfy yourself that the advantages outweigh the disadvantages.

Franchising is an increasingly popular and easy way of getting into your own business. You invest in a new 'branch' of a business that is already established. You will get considerable support from the franchisor with all the advantages of a proven product or service, but the rewards are limited by the franchise agreement. Franchisors normally exert a high degree of control over the franchise operation, although the franchisee is legally independent. Franchises can be expensive, involving fees for continuing support provided by the franchisor. Make thorough enquiries about any franchise and ask for independent legal advice before committing yourself to a contract.

Networking with business associates is an informal approach to leveraging advantage. Your business remains under your control, but you build relationships with others in the same kind of business to share the costs of marketing and perhaps of delivery. This approach has no legal foundation, unless you enter into specific contracts with associates. It depends upon the trust you build up with your associates. Networking can lead to a wider range of customers and to the growth of your business. You must be prepared, however, to give as well as to take.

Don't underestimate your liability. Sole traders and partnerships have unlimited liability for the debts of the business, therefore personal assets could be at risk. Limited companies must comply with a wide range of complex and detailed legislation, which can add to the administrative and financial burden.

While limited companies must legally have employers' liability insurance, it is also recommended for some businesses to have professional indemnity (PI) or public liability (PL) insurance. Speak to your accountant or financial adviser if you are in any doubt.

Periodically review your choice as you can usually change to another legal entity later, as your business develops. Your choice will affect the tax you pay, so get advice from an accountant.

7 Check your ability to cope with the pressure of running a business

To run your own business, of whatever kind, you need not only capital and capability, but also flair, toughness and good fortune. Managing a business is not an easy option. Many start-up businesses fail in the first few years, often as a result of poor preparation. Many other businesses do not make a profit until the third or fourth year of trading, and it can take many long hours of work to get to that stage. Do you have what it takes to succeed, and will you enjoy it?

Measure yourself against the following criteria (preferably on a scale of 1–5, 1 being low and 5 being high):

- I am self-disciplined
- I do not let things drift
- I have the full support of my family
- I can cope under pressure
- I am ready to work long hours and outside normal office hours, if necessary
- I am self-motivated
- I get on well with people and I can motivate them
- I can make quick decisions when they are needed
- I persist when the going gets tough
- I can learn from mistakes and I can take advice
- I am patient and I don't expect quick results
- I am in good health, enthusiastic and aware of the risks
- I am focused and have clear aims, including the need to look after myself and my family.

If you do not score well on these criteria (at least 3 on every item), take another look at your reasons for wanting to set up your own business.

8 Draw up a business plan

Whatever kind of business you are planning to start, it is important to undertake a disciplined planning process. This should be done even if you are funding the start-up from your own resources, and certainly if you aim to raise capital externally. The first step is to prove that the business idea is sound and that the start-up you are contemplating is financially viable. Produce a set of objectives and make them SMART (specific, measurable, achievable, realistic and time-specific).

Many banks provide advice on drawing up business plans. Consult more than one local branch to see what they can offer. Even if you don't need bank funding, you do need a business plan – and you can only benefit from a banker's views on the plan you produce.

As an entrepreneur you should avoid:

- making any important decisions until you have talked them through with family, friends, advisers such as accountants and lawyers, and those who have 'been there already'

- trying to set up a business just because it 'looks like a good idea'

- overstretching financial resources – borrowed money has to be repaid, usually with interest

- assuming that being your own boss is easy

- starting a business for the wrong reasons

- failing to admit to mistakes – do not simply brush them under the carpet, learn from them

- underestimating the competition.

Setting up as a consultant

The Management Consultancy Competence Framework developed by the Institute of Business Consulting, now the Institute of Consulting, defines consultancy as follows:

Management consulting involves individuals, whether self-employed or employed, using their knowledge and experience, and their analytical and problem-solving skills, to add value into a wide variety of organisations within a framework of appropriate and relevant professional standards, disciplines and ethics.

Consultancy usually involves the identification and assessment of a problem or the analysis of a specific area of an organisation, the reporting of findings and the formulation of recommendations for improvement. Consultants are commonly called in for business improvement, change management, information technology and long-term planning projects.

Setting up as an independent consultant is a popular career option for experienced managers or professionals who are looking for a fresh challenge, are attracted by the prospect of running their own business, or are seeking a second career or alternative employment after redundancy. Consultancy can offer varied assignments, the ability to choose interesting work, and the flexibility (within limits) of deciding when and where to work. At the same time, independent consultants may miss the security of a regular income and a company benefits package, suffer isolation and reduced job security, or face difficulties in maintaining their work–life balance. These issues should be considered carefully before starting out on your own.

This checklist provides initial guidance on the process of finding clients and carrying out consultancy assignments, rather than the legal and administrative aspects of setting up a business.

Action checklist

1 Identify your area of expertise or specialisation

Decide what kind of consultancy services you will offer. Describing yourself as a 'management' consultant may be too broad if you are setting up on your own. It is important to have a generalist understanding of all areas of the business, but you need to identify your specific marketing proposition and draw up a mission statement. Identify the reasons clients should work with you and how you will be able to help them. Consider your strengths and weaknesses – by carrying out a SWOT analysis, for example – and choose one or two areas of specialisation based on your experience.

2 Carry out market research

Consider what your market is, what it could be in the future, and how you will get access to it. Find out what opportunities there are within your chosen specialist areas. These might involve filling a gap in regional or market coverage, or providing a higher-quality or more personal service at a lower cost.

You need to assess:

- the market for your specialisation and the extent to which it is already being satisfied
- competitors – research their products and services and customers' views of them
- threats to existing markets and opportunities for new markets.

If you are not already a member, consider joining a professional organisation such as the UK-based Institute of Consulting, which offers networking opportunities and market resources to members.

If the market appears small or overcrowded, think about other ways in which your knowledge or experience could be used. Be wary of trying to compete on price alone or of setting up at all if you cannot identify something you can provide that is not already being offered cost-effectively. If necessary, repeat the market research process until you can identify promising opportunities or directions.

3 Work out a charging strategy

Research market rates in your specialist area and the relevant geographical market. Information on fees is not always easy to obtain. Skillfair does an annual survey of rates in the UK, with breakdowns by region and area of specialism.

Offer a discount on the market rates to:

- compensate clients for the risk in employing you rather than an established firm

- reflect your lower overheads.

Do not charge too low a rate, however, as it is difficult to raise rates later if you discount heavily at first. Remember, too, that clients like to feel they are receiving advice that is good value rather than cheap. Clients are suspicious of cut-price consultancy.

Calculate a realistic number of fee-earning days. Allow time for holidays (including public holidays), sickness, marketing your services, and attending courses and networking events. Bear in mind, too, that not all working days will be billable to consulting projects. Some experts suggest that 110 days is an acceptable number.

You could also offer to carry out one or two projects per year on a 'pro bono' basis, to show others what you can do.

4 Plan your marketing strategy

- List your particular selling points. Put yourself in the position of a client trying to decide whether to employ you rather than an established consultant.

- Register with consultancy directories and agencies.

- Join a professional organisation, network or other professional group.

- Register with directories such as the National Consultants' Register run by the Institute of Consulting. This is open to members and non-members.

- Write papers or books for publication or presentation at a conference.

- Give talks to appropriate local groups.

- Get in touch with recent contacts and use your network.

- Put together a printed package for distribution to potential clients, including your business card and details of your areas of expertise.

- Develop your own website.

- Create a list of consultants in other business areas, with a view to cooperating on a project as the opportunity arises.

- Ask to be introduced to decision-makers in organisations you would like to work with.

- Once you have the required level of experience, consider becoming a Certified Management Consultant. This qualification is awarded by national professional bodies for management consultancy recognised by the International Council of Management Consulting Institutes (see: www.icmci.org/certified_management_consultant). In the UK, this is the Institute of Consulting (see www.iconsulting.org.uk/training_and_qualifications/cmc).

5 Find your first client

Before you do anything else, find your first client. If you do not have a contract or a potential contract from a former employer, trawl every existing business contact.

Securing the first client will:

- make it easier for you to market to prospective new clients
- firm up your ideas about the type of business you want to become
- provide income.

6 Write the proposal

A winning proposal needs to demonstrate:

- knowledge of and experience in the area in question
- understanding of the client's requirements
- a creative and innovative approach to the project.

A comprehensive approach will include the following steps:

- providing evidence of the factors listed above
- carrying out research – consulting key people as well as gathering information from published sources
- setting out clearly the purpose and scope of the project
- demonstrating creativity – in setting out ideas and possible solutions
- giving details of your USP (unique selling point) – what sets you apart from the rest
- addressing the competition – not by emphasising their weaknesses, but by focusing on your strengths
- clarifying your strategy – where you will take the client and how you will get them there
- estimating costs and proposing budgets
- explaining the benefit of the project to the client – being as

specific as you can (for example, this project will increase profitability by 4%)

- presenting the proposal so as to get the attention of the readers
- producing a summary and placing it at the beginning of the document
- writing objectively, clearly and simply.

If possible, ask a friend or colleague to review your draft proposal. This will give you an objective perspective on the proposal. Then make any amendments or clarifications as necessary.

7 Negotiate the contract

Reaching agreement on the contract is the crucial stage, securing your client and determining the nature of the work to be done. The contract will also specify how you will be paid – by performance, percentage or daily rate – and what kind of expenses will be permissible. You will need negotiating skills to reach the agreement you want; there are always some areas for adjustment, just as there may also be some which are non-negotiable. It is important to be able to 'read' these in advance. Don't allow yourself to appear greedy, but don't undervalue your skills either.

8 Conduct the assignment

Key steps to success include:

- keeping to budget and time
- sticking to the purpose and scope of the project – avoiding scope creep
- understanding the client's organisational culture and language
- ensuring relevant staff are involved and consulted
- holding regular feedback sessions with your client
- maintaining an ethical and professional approach at all times.

As a consultant you should avoid:

● being tempted to set up a business or incur costs before securing the first client

● underestimating the costs of setting up or the delays in receiving payments from clients

● forgetting to ensure that work is covered by professional indemnity insurance

● sitting and waiting for someone to call. You may be the best in your field but you need to make sure that potential clients know about you – a proactive approach is required.

Planning your retirement

Retirement may mean the end of paid employment, but with increased longevity and better health many more people can now look forward to twenty years or more in retirement. This is a large slice of life that needs to be planned for, so that it can be as comfortable and enjoyable as possible. Planning, particularly financial planning, needs to be long term.

Patterns of employment are changing, and long service with a single or even a number of employers right through to normal retirement age is no longer the norm. Early retirement, part-time working and self-employment are becoming increasingly popular. Many wish to maintain their independence, building up a portfolio of work through interim jobs, consultancy, part-time training, writing and non-executive directorships, to name but a few. Although this is acknowledged, this checklist is intended primarily for those currently in employment who are starting to consider the impact of 'conventional' retirement.

Good retirement planning should start early to enable you to enjoy many active and satisfying years after your retirement. This new phase in your life can then be approached with confidence. Anxieties about money can be alleviated and you will be able to look forward to new experiences, perhaps developing yourself in ways that you had not had the opportunity to explore before. It is important to consider what you want to get out of your retirement. You will have more time available to pursue your own interests, be they hobbies, voluntary work, or part-time work. Think about the balance you want to achieve between these different types of pursuits.

The age of retirement is increasingly a matter of personal choice. In the UK, for example, the legally imposed default retirement age of 65 has been abolished.

Action checklist

1 Adopt a positive attitude

Growing older is something that happens to everyone. Retirement allows you to make a fresh start and adopt a new way of life, and should be welcomed rather than feared. However, it helps to be aware of any potential problems beforehand and to make sensible plans.

2 Plan your finances

One of the commonest fears about retirement is whether there will be enough money to enjoy it. You will want to aim to maintain the standard of living in retirement that you had during your working life. Do take advantage of any pre-retirement counselling or courses offered by your employer.

You need to know your likely retirement income:

- If you belong to a company pension scheme, find out how much income this will provide. You should receive regular statements from your employer. If you have changed employers, you should make sure you have statements on any earlier entitlements you may have. It is likely that you will have the option of taking part of the pension as a lump sum. However, there are a number of factors to be taken into account when deciding on your best option and it would be prudent to take advice from an expert. If you are reinvesting the sum, will the yield from the investment, and the protection of your capital, be as good as the pension income sacrificed?

- Find out how much your state retirement pension is likely to be.

In the UK, you can get a state pension forecast from the Pension Service, part of the Department of Work and Pensions.

If you start planning early, for example ten years before retirement, you may be able to improve your position. You should make sure you are aware of any potential options open to you such as Additional Voluntary Contributions (AVCs).

If you have a partner, look at the position jointly. It is important to keep up-to-date with changes, particularly in taxation. It may, for example, be advantageous for the partner with the lower income to hold a larger slice of the investments. Your financial planning must take taxation into account and you should ensure you have at least an elementary knowledge of allowances, the tax bands and the position of your partner. Consider how much of your pension your partner might be entitled to in the event of your earlier death and whether this will be adequate. Also consider how much of your partner's pension you might be entitled to in the event that your partner dies earlier.

Consider what you will do if your pension fund collapses. Would it be prudent to build up some additional source of income that is independent of your pension fund?

Unless you are an expert, it is helpful to have an independent financial adviser who is not tied to the products of a particular investment house.

3 Make a will

Retirement is a good time to check your will and make sure it is still appropriate. If you have not already made a will, retirement is a good time to do so. Dying intestate can make things difficult for your beneficiaries. You can draw up a will yourself but there are pitfalls, and most people will want to seek advice from a qualified person. If you wish to pass on substantial sums to your beneficiaries, you may consider bequeathing some earlier to avoid death duties. Having made your will, make sure your executors and partner (or close relatives) know where it is kept.

4 Cater for the even older generation

With improved health and diet people are living longer. Upon retirement, you may find yourself with responsibility for, or the need to help, your parents or elderly relatives. They may need you to help move them into some form of sheltered housing, assist in managing their affairs or help them obtain the benefits to which they are entitled. Again, forethought and planning can make a difference.

5 Plan where you are going to live

You may dream of retiring to a favourite holiday spot, returning to the place where you grew up, moving nearer to your children or moving abroad. If you are considering moving, visit your chosen location and view it at its worst, considering the downsides as well as the upsides of relocating. It may seem the ideal location to begin with, but think about what it will be like as you get older. Consider health needs: an isolated village life may seem ideal until a hospital stay is required. When deciding upon your residence, think about whether you want to be near your family and friends, and the effect of moving away from familiar territory.

If you decide to remain in your existing residence, take a critical look at your home. Is it too big? People often think something smaller would be good for retirement, but you will be there all the time. Is there room for your planned leisure activities? Do you need a home office? Is it economical to run? Think about improvements or changes, such as the upkeep of your garden, so that you can still maintain it in twenty years' time.

6 Plan for your leisure and health

You have spent around 2,000 hours a year at work and this may at first seem a daunting time to fill. You may want to think about some part-time work, at least to start with, particularly if you are retiring early. There is an increasing demand for the skills of older people on a short-term or part-time basis. The essential element is to be flexible in your approach.

Short-term or part-time earnings will affect your tax position, so you should check this when accepting a job or assignment. They will not, however, affect your entitlement to your organisational or state pension.

There is unlimited scope for those who wish to give their time to voluntary work. Check out any local organisations, such as the Council for Volunteer Services or Voluntary Action, which can provide information about needs and opportunities in the local community. Many national organisations also appreciate help at local level and your management skills and experience are likely to be welcomed.

If you want to exercise your brain, there are many opportunities for learning through both correspondence and residential courses. Look at several different brochures to gain an idea of the options available.

Make sure you have plenty of social contacts. Even if you have a partner, each of you should have your own social life to avoid the danger of boring one another. Many people plan to spend more time developing a personal hobby or pastime during retirement. However, a pastime that sustained your interest during your spare time while in employment may not hold such an appeal for weeks, months, or even years during retirement. If you don't have a specific hobby or interest, try to cultivate one, particularly one that involves physical exercise. Walking and cycling are two examples, and both can be linked well with other hobbies such as photography, sketching or birdwatching. Consider the cost implications, if there are any, of the hobby or interest you wish to pursue to make certain that you are able to support it financially.

Have a health check on or before retirement. At best, this will reassure you; at worst, it will guide you as to what you should and shouldn't do. You may have had the benefit of private medical insurance as an employee or this might be something you paid for out of earnings. Think about whether you will be able to afford to continue with this after retirement, or whether your future needs can be met by the national health services.

7 Plan holidays

Holidays are just as important in retirement as before. But now you have greater freedom as to when you take them and can take advantage of off-peak prices. Check your home insurance to make sure you are covered if you are away for more than 30 days and ask someone to keep an eye on your property. It may also be worthwhile to look at specialist operators to see the range of holidays on offer. Consider taking out an annual travel insurance policy if you are likely to take a number of holidays each year.

8 Adjust

The changes in routine on a day-to-day basis that retirement brings will need a period of adaptation. Give yourself adequate time to adjust, so that you can begin to plan, and enjoy, this next phase of your life.

You should avoid:

- making hasty and potentially unwise decisions about finance or where to live

- worrying about finances – instead take a proactive approach to planning and start the process early

- worrying about how to fill your time.

Managing your time effectively

Time management is the conscious control of the amount of time spent on work activities in order to maximise personal efficiency. It involves analysing how time is spent, and then prioritising different work tasks. Activities can be reorganised to concentrate on those that are most important, and various techniques can be of help in carrying out tasks more quickly and efficiently. These include information-handling skills, verbal and written communication skills, delegation and daily time planning.

Effective time management is simply making the best use of limited time, which involves using your time to achieve the best possible goals. It can help you to gain more control over your activities, increase your efficiency, improve your work–life balance and become proactive rather than reactive in preventing or dealing with problems. Getting to grips with time management should help to reduce work pressures so that you will feel more relaxed, and others will be more likely to perceive you as calm and well organised.

Action checklist

1 Establish how your time is spent

Look back through your diary or log sheet to work out how you spend your time. If you have not done so, log your activities for a period of two weeks to see where your time is going.

Ask yourself:

- how much of your activity was a result of planning and how much was unplanned
- how accurate your planning was – did you complete tasks in the time allowed
- how much time you spent on routine activities which could be delegated
- how often interruptions diverted you from your tasks
- during which period of the day you tend to accomplish the most.

Use the grid below to establish which tasks or activities are urgent, important, non-urgent and not important.

Group A Urgent and important tasks	Group B Urgent and not important tasks
Group C Not urgent and important tasks	Group D Not urgent and not important tasks

2 Determine your problem areas

What is making you use time inefficiently? Split the problems into the 'enemy without' and the 'enemy within'. The enemy without includes external factors beyond your immediate control, such as the mistakes or inefficiencies of other departments, unexpected extra tasks and complaints. The enemy within is personal inefficiency, and includes poor planning, lack of assertiveness in turning away unwanted callers, and putting off problems and unenjoyable activities.

3 Be clear on your objectives and priorities

Before you can successfully manage your time, you must make sure that you are familiar with your job description and what you should and should not be doing as part of your job. Agree your precise role, objectives and targets with your superiors and your subordinates, so that everyone knows what is expected of you. This should be put in writing.

4 Tackle the enemy without

If you find that problem relationships, complaints and reacting to situations beyond your control take up too much of your time, try to minimise this by:

- setting service-level agreements detailing what each department expects from others and improving interdepartmental communication
- reviewing complaints procedures and setting up a more efficient system
- examining personnel policies which might be giving rise to interpersonal tension or inefficient work practices
- asking colleagues to be concise when giving written or oral reports.

5 Tackle the enemy within

Make more constructive use of your time.

Planning

- Map out your activities a week in advance.
- Spend five minutes each morning reviewing your time, and readjust your plan as circumstances change.
- Build slack time into your schedule so that you do not constantly overrun.
- Have a back-up plan for contingency situations – decide which tasks can be dropped, who can be called on to help out, and who will need to be notified if you are consequently delayed with other activities.
- Plan time for relaxation and recreation as well as work.

Prioritising

- Rank tasks in order of importance – try to be objective and avoid ranking highly those tasks that you enjoy the most but that are not crucial.

- Be firm but polite in refusing to undertake tasks that are not your responsibility.

- Maintain clear objectives on what you are trying to achieve and allocate your time accordingly.

Delegating

- Assess which tasks can be delegated to someone else.

- Choose carefully who you delegate to. Is the person knowledgeable and competent, and do they have the time and willingness to do the task? Will you offend anyone?

- Make sure you give clear instructions so that delegated tasks are done well.

- Involve others in projects and share the workload.

- Train your employees to manage their time effectively too.

Reviewing how you work

- Plan to do important activities at the time of day when you function best.

- Break down complex tasks into manageable chunks.

- Avert unwanted interruptions. If necessary, ask your secretary to ward off unwanted callers, work somewhere other than your office, or simply put a 'do not disturb' sign on the door (and make sure that people know it means what it says).

- Work at home for a day occasionally, if this is allowed and if home is a quiet environment.

- Talk to people instead of writing – this can result in a quicker response and quicker decision-making.

- Avoid task hopping – concentrate on one thing at a time.

- Batch similar tasks together.

- Take breaks or switch tasks when you feel tired or have a mental block.

- Keep accurate records and an organised filing system to save time locating information or having to compile documents again.

● Make use of new technology – but only if it really saves time.

● Minimise paperwork and avoid unnecessary duplication.

● Make sure the meetings you attend are necessary and, if running one yourself, make sure it is well organised.

● Look at your travel arrangements for commuting or work trips – can you eliminate or shorten unnecessary journeys?

6 Make time to play

Overwork is counter-productive. It can cause stress and affect the time efficiency you have worked so hard to achieve. However well organised you are, there are only 24 hours in a day and you need to devote an adequate proportion of them to yourself. Don't be afraid to take ten minutes for a tea break or a walk around the park, or an hour to go to the gym. Try to maintain a healthy work–life balance.

7 Make time to think

Quality thinking time (for example, when writing important plans or policies), free from interruption, is important as it provides the opportunity for reflection. In an open-plan office you could have a flag on your desk showing whether you can be interrupted or not.

As a manager you should avoid:

● wasting time on less important tasks when really important ones need doing

● procrastinating on dealing with problems that may worsen if they are ignored

● forgetting to take time for personal development

● neglecting your family, social life or relaxation activities.

Handling information: avoiding overload

For the purposes of this checklist, 'information' is used in its widest sense and includes written and oral, formal and informal communications. Many different skills are needed to handle information overload effectively, including the organisation and delivery of information.

Worldwide access to the internet has dramatically increased the availability of information, and its abundance can make it difficult to distinguish its quality or worth. Managers need to restrict the amount of information they access to a manageable level, balancing external, general and public information (such as business, political and economic news reports) with internal sources that are specific, tailored and usually private. Too much information causes anxiety and inefficiency, and insufficient information can lead to ineffective decision-making, management by guesswork and adverse consequences for business.

Controlling the flow of information requires a disciplined, informed and consistent approach to selection and evaluation. This checklist is for those who are concerned with the ever-increasing amount of information they are required to handle and describes a structured approach to controlling information overload.

Action checklist

1 Know yourself

People differ in their capacity to handle information, so it is worthwhile considering how much information you feel comfortable coping with at any one time. Establish how you deal with the various methods of recording information. Do you write notes of conversations or rely on memory? Are you able to make mental links between related pieces of information, or do you need a more formal system such as an index to help you find the relevant details? Be aware that information may be found on demand (when you search for it) or appear serendipitously (when a colleague tells you something in passing), and that both are valid and important.

2 Manage your time

If information swamps you continuously, set aside some time each day or week for activities such as the evaluation of information. Stick to the time limits you set.

Think about:

- how much time is available
- how flexible this is
- how much time can be spent on information processing
- how you work – do you take a break from a sustained task each time an email arrives?

3 Focus on objectives

Focus on current objectives, otherwise the information you accumulate under the umbrella 'may be useful at some time in the future' could quickly overwhelm you. It is important to define objectives and priorities – for information purposes – in terms of 'must have', 'nice to have' and 'not necessary for me to keep'. Concentrate on what you need to know, not on what might be nice to know. When there is time pressure these objectives will contract; occasionally there will be time for them to expand.

Must have includes information which:

- meets defined objectives
- is task-oriented
- relates to needs
- fits a designated purpose
- provides knowledge and understanding that will progress activities.

Nice to have includes information which:

- might be useful one day
- is unsolicited but of interest.

Not necessary is often obvious but also includes information which:

- is easily obtainable on demand
- will not cause any damage if missed.

4 Choose access and delivery methods

Choosing access and delivery methods is important throughout any cycle of information control. The medium can influence the message or drown it if we are not careful. All information sources consume time in different ways:

- libraries of printed materials can take time to sift and sort through
- database or internet searches can leave you with hundreds of references and it can be time-consuming to narrow these down to the most relevant
- internet portals or communities promise to provide all you need on a subject but may end up by flooding you with masses of unedited data
- a message sent by email for convenience may involve printing out a large number of pages.

Libraries have the benefit of being systematically organised – be especially wary of information sources that are not organised.

Choose your medium with care, or you may end up with too much poor-quality information which will need culling. Keep objectives and selection criteria firmly in mind. Familiarise yourself with sources of information and learn how to use them; you will then be able to retrieve information more effectively when you need it.

5 Establish selection criteria

We either deal with information as soon as it arrives because it is something on which we need to act, or:

- pass it on to someone else – this may just be passing the problem on rather than solving it, unless you know that the recipient has a need for it
- save it for a rainy day – this means that you will become weighed down with clutter which takes time to organise, and may not give a profitable return on the effort invested in it (not even the largest of electronic libraries can hold everything you might need)
- get rid of it – this is often the only sensible, practical option.

Asking the following questions should help determine which of these is the best course of action:

- Do I need this now? Can I use it on a current project?
- Where does this come from? Is the source reliable, reputable, authoritative?
- Did I ask for it? If it hadn't arrived, would I have gone looking for it?
- Is it speculative, substantiated or controversial? Is it directly about the subject in question?
- Is it worth keeping for the future? Could I get hold of it again if needed?
- Is it worth passing to someone else?

6 Gain confidence in what you know

We do not know what we do not know. However, when we read new material in the hope of finding new ideas, we may discover that we are aware of most of the contents and reading it has not added to the sum of our knowledge, although this may perhaps be helpful in reassuring us that we are up-to-date.

It is important to get an idea of how often this happens, and how frequently something striking and worthwhile comes your way. This might provide you with your own 80–20 rule. Allied with your knowledge of proven/best/reliable/innovative sources, this may help you cut down the quantities of repeat information heaped upon you.

7 Consult

Often a face-to-face conversation is worth a thousand memos and reports – it is a question of investing initial time to make savings later. Your colleagues are probably your best source of information, but they should be supplemented by a group of experts you can trust to help you cut your way through to what you really need. This may include a professional body, specialised library, government department or government-sponsored information and advice service. If you want to get to grips with a new subject, get hold of a summary article, digest or checklist from a reputable source.

Most organisations have 'gatekeepers': people who gather large quantities of information and are good communicators. These people can help you sift and filter information. Find your own gatekeeper if you don't have one already.

8 Be ruthless with paperwork

- Remove your name selectively from external and internal mailing lists.

- Ask colleagues to report by exception, and then to be concise – a one-page management summary, for example.

- Return unnecessary paperwork to the sender, or bin it.

- If you can use someone else as a sifter, do so – but make sure this does not result in them being overloaded as well.

9 Be ruthless with electronic data, especially on the internet

● Work out personal screening procedures, for example culling information by source or origin.

● Use software that ranks content by relevance, rather than scanning through hundreds of documents.

● Don't pass on messages which might be of use; give them only to those who you know will be interested.

● Remember to use the delete key. With too much dross there is a swift, though final, answer.

● If important information comes to you from the internet, consider using feeds or similar ways to get information 'pushed' to you instead of spending time looking for it.

● Be wary, however, of subscribing to numerous open e-newsletters or discussion groups, where comments are circulated to everyone.

As a manager you should avoid:

● becoming a slave to routine activities which have lost pertinence

● tolerating unsolicited rubbish

● dealing with a piece of paper more than once.

Solving problems

A problem is the distance between how things are and how they should be. Problem-solving is the 'bridge' between these two elements. To close the gap, you need to understand how things are (problem) and how they ought to be (solution).

Although there is a clear distinction between problem-solving and decision-making, the two are often used interchangeably. Problem-solving differs fundamentally from decision-making. A problem occurs when something is not behaving as it should, something is deviating from the norm, something goes wrong. Decision-making is a case of choosing between different alternatives; it is required in response to the question: 'Which computer shall I buy?' Problem-solving is needed in response to the statement: 'My computer won't work.'

Problem-solving is a valuable skill that can be learnt, and perfected, through continual practice. There are a wide range of problem-solving models and techniques available to help solve diverse problems of varying degrees of severity. The purpose of this checklist is not to recommend a specific model; rather it is to act as a guide to the generic problem-solving process. You are encouraged to find the model that best works for you – one that is flexible and can be adapted to suit your specific circumstances. Over time, your model of choice should become an automatic and integral part of your working practices. However, it is important to understand the limitations of your model.

Most problem-solving methods follow a common pattern, beginning with a definition of the problem, moving on to the consideration of potential solutions, and culminating with the selection, testing and implementation of a course of action. Divergent thinking techniques can be helpful in generating creative ideas, while convergent thinking can assist in structuring and evaluating potential solutions.

Problems can be classified into one of two categories: the 'fix-it' or 'do-it':

- Fix-it – solving an existing problem (for example, a product range is falling short of its sales targets). An immediate short-term solution could be to increase marketing activity.

- Do-it – moving you in the right direction for what you want to achieve (for example, a new product range needs to be introduced to compete with market rivals). This type of problem will require longer-term planning to achieve its objective.

Irrespective of the severity or complexity of the problem, the process should:

- be systematic and thorough
- provide evidence to show how the problem was solved
- prevent a rush to a solution without understanding the cause of the problem
- enable possible causes to be assessed.

Action checklist

1 Define and understand the problem

Once you have been made aware of and identified the problem, investigate what has gone wrong. Try to identify the problem through signals from routine statistical returns, progress meetings, suggestion schemes, reports and feedback. A rising tide of complaints, for example, could stem from faulty machinery, poor packaging, staff absence, poor staff training, product deficiency, false marketing hype, and so on. Getting the definition accurate is crucial. Otherwise you might find that you are solving the wrong problem. If the problem is not correctly defined, a satisfactory solution is unlikely.

2 Assess the scale of the problem

Decide how urgent the problem is and how soon it requires solving. Is it a top priority or can it wait for a few weeks, months or even years? Consider the implications if the problem isn't resolved immediately. What are the consequences? It might be an urgent problem, but it might not be important in the grand scheme of things. Think strategically and consider whether a quick solution (fix-it) or an optimal solution (do-it) is required. This will determine the scale of the problem and its related solution.

3 Gather relevant information

To get a full picture of the problem, it is essential to gather all the relevant information – everything that may have an influence on the problem. Get details of the people, activities, processes, equipment, systems and timescales involved and the conditions in which the problem occurs. Tap into other resources at your disposal such as data held by your IT systems. Gather the critical facts by asking the right questions of the right people, namely the what, why, how, where, who and when.

- What is the problem? For example, orders not being processed for product line X

- What is not the problem? For example, orders for product lines Y & Z

- Where is the problem located? For example, on the shop-floor

- Where is the problem not located? For example, administration

- Why is the problem occurring? For example, labour shortage

- When is the problem in evidence? For example, during the early morning shift

- When is the problem not in evidence? For example, during the afternoon and late shift

- Who is affected by it? For example, departmental manager, shop-floor staff
- Who is not affected by it? For example, clerical, administrative staff
- What is different about those affected? For example, a rise in absenteeism, job dissatisfaction
- What things are affected by the problem? For example, meeting production targets, customer satisfaction
- What things are not affected? For example, machine capacity.

Identify and talk to those directly involved. Others may be better placed than you in determining the cause of the problem. Be selective in the information and facts you gather to avoid overload. Too much information may hide crucial details and result in important clues being overlooked.

4 Identify the root causes

Armed with the facts, you need to make sure you understand the root cause of the problem. Causes usually relate to people, systems or equipment. Be careful not to blame the tool when it could be the operator. Asking the right questions will help to identify the cause:

- When did the problem first occur? For example, 6–7 weeks ago
- What changed? For example, a staff member left
- What changes might be relevant? For example, recruit more staff or reposition existing staff.

Distinguish the symptoms from the root cause: where does it occur, when does it occur, who is involved, what is the precise problem? To identify the root cause, keep asking why until a satisfactory answer is found.

5 Test the hypothesis

Once you have identified a likely cause, work out a hypothesis to test exactly what it is you are looking for and how you will know if you are right. The cause of a problem is always a change from the norm that has produced effects in some places but not in others. Look at the information you assembled in points 1–4 to test, on paper, whether the cause finds a good match with how, where and when the problem occurs, to what extent it occurs and who is affected by it.

6 Involve others

Don't assume that it is up to you to solve every problem. Ascertain whose responsibility it is and delegate to others if appropriate. This may include hiring external experts to seek outside assistance. Involve key players and talk through possible solutions and decisions with other people. Hold a brainstorming meeting to examine all the available solutions. The solution is the outcome you want to achieve. Consider all suggestions put forward by the group, giving each idea due consideration. Avoid pitfalls such as failing to consider all the options, focusing exclusively upon one solution, or sticking with the 'tried and tested' solutions of yesteryear.

7 Consider the proposed solution(s)

Don't be swayed by people with ready-made solutions. There may be a number of possible solutions, some of which might be more appropriate than others. This is the time to move from problem analysis to a method for decision-making. Think about the consequences and outcomes of your problem-solving decisions. Will the proposed action resolve the issue effectively, or will further action be needed later? Assess the risks by contemplating what could go wrong. What impact, if any, will the proposed solution have on other areas? And how serious would the consequences be? Consider as many possible scenarios as you can to eradicate any solutions that simply won't work. Also, consider all possible constraints for implementation such as money, resources, time and operational limitations.

Resist the temptation to be impetuous and take action without first taking time to reflect. Acting too quickly without due consideration of your options might lead to additional problems further down the line. Bear in mind that there may not be an ideal solution, but there should be a 'best' one (even if 'best' means 'better than the rest').

8 Test the proposed solution

Once a consensus has been reached, the idea needs to be tested. This can be done mentally or physically depending upon feasibility. Mentally assess the idea by presenting different scenarios and seeing how the proposed solution performs. Or, if possible, pilot the solution to test its merits in a practical setting. When you are satisfied that the solution has been adequately tested and holds up to the assessment criteria, produce a plan showing a schedule of actions and by whom and when they are to be carried out.

9 Champion your decision

To implement it within the organisation, your proposed solution will undoubtedly require some resources, such as financial or human resources. If additional resources are required, it may be necessary to present your case to senior management for approval. Choose a method of presenting the facts that others can understand: a SWOT analysis, for example. Champion your idea with confidence to make things happen. In tough economic times, you will be competing for scarce resources. Maximise your chances of success by focusing on the benefits of your idea – whether short term or long term – to the business. Consider the timing of your communication carefully to maximise the prospects of a positive response, for example before the year's budget has been allocated, or before the cost of fixing the problem is too great to be resourced.

10 Monitor the results

Once the solution has been found and implemented, don't rest on your laurels. Instead, monitor the impact of the changes made. The problem is truly solved only when the solution is translated into successful action. Keep monitoring the results and reassessing the situation to prevent and/or anticipate any future problems. Decisions should be open-ended and subject to constant review in the ever-changing marketplace. The solution to a problem need not necessarily become routine practice. Continue to test and review its effectiveness to make sure it is still the best available. If the problem still isn't resolved, begin the whole process again – but don't repeat the same mistakes and steer clear of any pitfalls.

As a manager you should avoid:

- neglecting to test possible causes against the data gathered
- taking on sole responsibility for the problem and the solution
- jumping to an apparently obvious solution without evidence
- forgetting to check on progress and ensure that the problem has been successfully resolved.

Making rational decisions

Decision-making is the process of choosing between alternative courses of action. It may take place at an individual or organisational level

This checklist outlines a process for making rational decisions and a simple decision-making framework is provided. It is therefore relevant to all managers.

The nature of the decision-making process within an organisation is influenced by its culture and structure, and a number of theoretical models have been developed. One well-known model for individual decision-making was put forward by Charles Kepner and Benjamin Tregoe in their book *The New Rational Manager* (published in 1981). Specific techniques used in decision-making include heuristics and decision trees. Computer systems designed to assist managerial decision-making are known as decision support systems.

The rational model for decision-making:

- will provide evidence and support for how the decision was made
- is particularly suitable for complex or fuzzy situations
- is thorough and systematic
- relies on effective information gathering, rather than preconceived ideas
- is an effective technique for determining a course of action and securing commitment to it.

It is worth noting that information-gathering should not be restricted to facts. Successful decision-making requires preconceptions and assumptions, the reasons they exist and how they are used to be identified and treated as valuable information.

There can, however, be drawbacks because this method:

- can be time-consuming and resource-intensive, especially in fast-moving situations
- relies heavily on information which may prove difficult to gather
- requires fairly strict adherence if the outcome is to be a rational decision
- highlights the possibility that a rational decision may not be the right one.

It is extremely useful and rational behaviour for managers not to ignore their gut feelings. But it is important to note that this is not equivalent to acting on those feelings.

Action checklist

1 Define the decision to be made

Be clear about the exact decision to make. This first step helps to clarify thinking, aids communications and provides a record for the future. It may lead to the discovery that assumptions made previously have muddied the water.

For example: a decision needs to be made regarding which computer to buy.

2 Establish the objectives

The objectives (which are not the same as goals) are the results that are desired from the decision and should be measurable wherever possible. At this stage it is not necessary to be concerned if there are apparent incompatibilities between objectives. Start by identifying all the stakeholders with an interest in the matter, which involves consultation, information-seeking and checking.

Your objective may be a computer that can access the internet anywhere, run CD-ROMs and DVDs, includes word-processing, spreadsheet and graphics software, has a large hard drive and is affordable. So the computer must have wireless internet access, USB ports, CD-ROM/DVD drive, adequate RAM, a large hard drive, standard software packages and be within budget.

3 Classify the objectives

Differentiate between the essential requirements (the 'musts') and the desirable ones (the 'wants'). The fundamental difference between 'musts' and 'wants' is that if one of the decision options does not meet a 'must', that option should be rejected. Failure to meet a 'want' should not mean automatic rejection. The process for considering 'wants' is dealt with in point 5.

Musts: maximum price, minimum RAM memory capacity, minimum hard-drive capacity

Wants: wireless internet access, CD-ROM/DVD drive, USB ports, software packages

4 Define the 'musts'

To be a valid 'must', an objective should have a quantitative measure or an objective standard. Assign quantitative measures to the 'musts': maximum price £600, minimum 1GB RAM memory, minimum 100GB hard drive. This means that if an option presented for purchase costs more than £600, has less than 1GB RAM or has a less than 100GB hard drive, it should be rejected.

5 Define the 'wants'

Examine the 'wants' for importance and give them a numerical weighting out of 10 (10 for the most important, less for the less important). For example, if the software packages are the most important feature after the 'musts', they should be weighted 10. If an option includes spreadsheet, database, graphics and word-processing, it may well score 10 out of 10; but if one element is missing, it may score only 8. An option with an extremely fast modem with built-in error correction may have a weight of 10; but one with a slower, less sophisticated modem may score only 6.

Wireless internet access	10
Complete software package	10
CD-ROM/DVD drive	9
Extra USB ports	8

6 Generate the options

Once the information requirements are established, you should obtain the appropriate information. In this case, sources may include computer suppliers, the trade press and 'informed' colleagues.

7 Apply the options to the requirements

The information obtained for each option should be recorded against each 'must' objective.

8 Test the options against the 'musts'

Reject options that do not meet the 'musts'. Check whether any of the other options fail to match the 'musts' on price, storage capacity or processor. If the answer is no, it is logical to reject that option.

If you do not wish to reject or something else prevents you from rejecting an option that has failed on 'musts', either the 'musts' are incorrect or you are not adhering to the rational process. In both cases, restart at point 3.

9 Score the remaining options against the 'wants'

Score the remaining options against each of the 'wants' in turn. The one that meets the 'want' best should be scored highest and the others allocated proportionate scores. For example:

Wireless internet access	6
2 out of 4 software elements missing	5

No CD-ROM/DVD drive   0
2 extra memory slots   8

10 Multiply the weights by the scores

Weights should be multiplied by scores and the results added for each option. For example, as in steps 5 and 9:

Wireless internet access	10×6	60
2 out 4 software elements missing	10×5	50
No CD-ROM/DVD	9×0	0
2 extra memory slots	8×8	64
Total		174

11 Make a provisional decision

The totals will enable you to make a provisional decision. With the totals compared it is usually possible to make statements such as:

- option A is clearly the best
- options D and E are not worth considering
- there is little to choose between options B and C.

12 The final decision

The analysis will not provide an automatic decision, unless all options but one fail the 'musts'. Where several options have similar totals, it is particularly important to re-examine scores and weights and the evidence on which they have been based. The analysis will provide a sound framework for clear examination. It is not always necessary to use the entire process described above, especially for simple binary (yes/no) decisions. However, each element in the process can be used separately to improve the efficiency of a decision. Some initial assumptions have to be made in the decision process. Make sure you review all the assumptions before proceeding to the analysis described above. In the computer example, a technological assumption made at the beginning is that you need a minimum of 1GB RAM. Once the assumption is made, it will condition your choice and you need to be sure the assumption is correct.

As a manager you should avoid:

- jumping too quickly to an apparently obvious decision
- letting a preconceived notion influence the process
- cutting corners, especially if the decision has far-reaching implications
- letting personal preferences cloud the process
- taking the provisional decision as final
- ignoring your instinct
- using this approach for solving problems.

Simple decision-making framework

For less complex decisions or when qualitative data are considered, you can use the following table.

Desired result		
Possible solution 1	Pros	Cons
Possible solution 2	Pros	Cons
Possible solution 3	Pros	Cons
Recommendation and rationale		

Stress management: self first

The UK Health and Safety Executive defines stress as 'the adverse reaction people have to excessive pressure or other types of demand placed on them'. Studies have shown that stress is closely related to the degree of control individuals have over their work – self-controlled pressure can be tolerated at a high level, while the threshold for imposed pressure is low. The experience of stress, therefore, is highly personal. Pressures come from many different directions, affecting us in different ways at different times.

In some situations when we are under an enormous amount of pressure, we cope, are stimulated and on occasion positively thrive. In other situations we may suffer in some way, show signs of not coping and feel unable to meet either the deadlines or the expectations. This is the experience of stress. Most people need a certain level of pressure to motivate them; it is when it gets beyond this level that problems arise.

Successive waves of reorganisation, downsizing, closure or expansion can put pressure on managers and employees alike. Technological changes that have improved the speed of communications in the form of smart mobile telephones, instant messaging and email have created twenty-four-hour accessibility and an increase in the pace of work. Coping with and adapting to these changes can be an immense challenge. The detrimental effects of poorly managed pressures can be measured in terms of the cost to organisations and society as a whole. Research carried out by the Labour Force Survey (LFS) indicates an estimated 10.4 million working days were lost in the UK in 2011/12 due to work-related stress.* The personal cost to individuals is less easy to measure but it can be enormous, and can affect quality of life and relationships.

This checklist is designed to help individuals recognise symptoms of stress and sources of pressure and identify coping strategies.

Action checklist

1 Recognise your symptoms

Symptoms can alert you to the fact that you may be under stress. Commonly experienced symptoms include:

- health – headaches, upset stomach, sleep problems, change in appetite, tense muscles, indigestion, exhaustion, stomach, intestinal and skin problems
- behaviour – feeling worried, irritated, demotivated, unable to cope and make decisions; being less creative; nail-biting; excessive smoking and/or use of alcohol
- work – lower job satisfaction, communication breakdown, a focus on unproductive tasks.

All these symptoms may be experienced in normal life; they become symptoms of stress only when several occur together, when they do not have an obvious cause, or when you experience them more often than you would expect. Also, although the symptoms are often exhibited in your workplace behaviour, they are not necessarily a reflection of workplace pressures.

2 Identify the sources

We live in an ever-changing world and must constantly adapt and adjust to technological and social changes. There are also

---

* Labour Force Survey, Health and Safety Executive: stress-related and psychological disorders, www.hse.gov.uk/statistics/causdis/stress/stress.pdf

recurring pressures that form a predictable pattern of events in our lives and can be a source of stress and satisfaction.

In everyday life these may include:

● the death of someone close

● divorce

● injury

● moving house

● a large mortgage

● holidays

● birth of a child (especially the first).

At work they may include:

● time pressures

● demanding deadlines

● relationships with others

● too much or too little work

● business or work changes

● threat of redundancy

● pressure from above

● insensitive management.

3 Know your response

Individuals respond to these external pressures by adapting and adjusting in a variety of ways, depending on their lifestyle. Two broad categories have been identified according to personality type. Type A people could be described as competitive, aggressive or hasty; Type B people are just the reverse. Type A people tend to take stress out on others; Type B people internalise it. Other characteristics such as age, gender, health, financial situation and access to support can influence how we respond to change, regardless of our personality traits.

4 Identify the strategies that help you cope

Individuals react differently to stress, so each has different coping strategies. Identify those that have been successful in the past. They may have involved:

- breaking up big problems into smaller, achievable goals
- readjusting your work–life balance
- removing or reducing outside pressure
- accepting the things that can't be changed.

5 Begin to make the necessary changes

Change yourself – you can be your own worst enemy:

- be realistic
- recognise your weaknesses and strengths
- talk to others, at home and at work – don't bottle up stress
- remember you are not the only one who is stressed – you are not alone.

Change relationships – they can be both supportive and damaging:

- invest in developmental and supportive relationships
- withdraw from damaging relationships.

Change activities – they create balance and an opportunity for release:

- relax, if necessary by using well established techniques
- develop interests that nourish you
- take sensible exercise – a great way to relieve tension
- eat well; eat a sensibly balanced diet
- get enough sleep to ensure you are refreshed.

Your happiness and well-being depend on making changes. When change comes, it will bring with it an easing of pressures, profound changes in personality and mood, and an approach to life that benefits you and those with whom you live and work.

As a manager you should avoid:

- thinking that stress equates to weakness – this is not the way to approach this problem

- keeping it to yourself – this can be detrimental to your health; ignoring it and thinking it will heal itself will solve nothing

- stopping all activities – this will give you more time to think and worry; doing something you enjoy is far more therapeutic.

Emotional intelligence

Emotional intelligence (EI) is the ability to perceive, and understand, your own feelings and those of others. First popularised by Daniel Goleman in the 1990s, EI involves recognising emotions and acting on them in a reflective and critical manner.

During the past decade or so, EI has been considered to be a strong contributory factor in personal success. Many successful people in all walks of life have been found to have high levels of EI, indicating that they can be expected to be good at both managing themselves and understanding others. There are lots of key success indicators besides EI, but EI is associated with the softer skills that are frequently emphasised as important for success in leadership and management. This has led some writers and consultants to stress the significance of EI as an indicator of potential.

A person with high EI is generally expected to be self-aware, to have strong self-control, to reflect on his or her feelings and behaviour, and to be able to empathise well with other people. Those with high EI resist impulsive, spur-of-the-moment reactions to emotions and instead base their actions on a reflective consideration of their feelings, the situation, and possible responses and their consequences. At work, the capacity to react on the basis of thought, informed by feeling, can much enhance interpersonal communication and people skills.

This checklist explains the concept of emotional intelligence, which is sometimes referred to as EQ or emotional quotient. It gives an overview of the basic principles and outlines why EI is relevant for managers. A brief EI indicator self-test is given at the end.

Action checklist

1 Understand the theories of emotional intelligence

People generally experience a range of positive and negative emotions in response to their conscious experiences and relationships, and this happens at work just as it does everywhere else. Some typical examples of emotion felt at work might be satisfaction, exhilaration, anger, frustration, pride and anxiety.

The phrase 'emotional intelligence' was first defined in the 1980s by two American psychologists, John D. Mayer and Peter Salovey. A third American psychologist, Daniel Goleman, later built on their work and his popular book, *Emotional Intelligence: Why It Can Matter More Than IQ*, included a five-element framework for emotional intelligence:

- **self-awareness** – the ability to understand yourself, your strengths and weaknesses, and how others see you

- **self-regulation** – the ability to control yourself and think before you act

- **motivation** – the drive to work and succeed

- **empathy** – the ability to understand other people's feelings and viewpoints

- **social skills** – communicating and relating to others.

Two other researchers associated with EI are Malcolm Higgs and Victor Dulewicz, who identified seven elements of EI that can be broken down into three main categories:

- **drivers** – motivation and decisiveness, traits that energise and drive people to meet high goals

- **constrainers** – conscientiousness/integrity and emotional resilience, traits that act as controls and curb the excesses of the drivers (especially if these are too high, undirected or misdirected)

- **enablers** – sensitivity, influence and self-awareness, traits that facilitate performance and success.

2 Emotional intelligence at work

When at work, many of us think we should try to ignore our emotional responses, especially if they are extreme or negative. EI, by contrast, involves recognising and understanding our emotions. When strong emotions such as anger, joy, fear, frustration, pleasure or anxiety are experienced, the human brain is programmed to respond instinctively. The response triggered is physical as well as emotional and includes heightened blood pressure and increased hormonal levels that, in primitive terms, prime us for immediate action of some sort: to fight in self-defence, jump for joy, shout, or run away, for example. At work, however, and in most modern contexts, such instinctive physical or verbal responses could well be inappropriate, and may lead people to say or do things they later regret.

People with high levels of EI recognise their emotions and understand when a state of physiological arousal is experienced; but they are able to take a step back from their feelings, reflect on the situation, and consider possible responses and outcomes. They are also able to recognise other people's emotions, appreciate their potential state of physical arousal, and (hopefully) help them avoid impulsive, negative reactions such as losing their temper or storming out of a difficult meeting.

3 Ask yourself how this applies to your role at work

Some particular management competencies depend strongly upon EI. To manage successfully, you need to be able to:

- manage yourself (self-regulation and constraints) and not vent any frustration you feel on colleagues
- be self-aware and recognise your real, rather than perceived, strengths and weaknesses

- seek feedback from others on your behaviour and actions, and reflect on them regularly
- recognise that everyone changes over time, and your work motivations and relationships will change too
- motivate others as well as yourself
- counsel or coach others within the organisation (social skills, enablers)
- encourage others and offer advice (social skills, enablers)
- develop good working relationships (empathy and enablers).

The need to consider action to develop EI is clear, if it is as important for leadership and management success as some theorists suggest, but there is some disagreement about whether it is possible to develop EI over the course of a lifetime. EI involves the ability to be empathetic and understand the perspectives of others. Although there is no empirical evidence for innate empathy, it is widely believed that empathetic abilities are usually shaped and developed early, during a person's childhood and adolescence.

It is generally accepted in psychology that emotional skills undergo lifelong development, just like any other skill, and some training approaches in perspective-taking and empathy have been developed that seem to have had some success with adults. Examples include the work of Robert Krauss at Columbia University, or the frequent use of empathy training in the re-socialisation of criminals. It is also recognised, however, that changes in empathy as a result of adult training will be slow and small. There may be no fast-track training approach for EI, but some related aspects, such as team-building and motivational skills, can be developed. There are also many books, seminars and courses that focus on such development, or at least aim to give a better understanding of the issues involved.

Until more academically rigorous and tested assessment outcomes are agreed, it is safe to assume that, at present, only some facets of EI can be learned or taught. Other facets –

adopting a more understanding attitude, or building drive and determination, for example – may be less open to supported development, and depend on individual experience, maturation and willingness to change.

4 Test and develop your emotional intelligence

The main problem when testing for EI is that there is no agreed, standard definition of the concept, and the range of characteristics and assessment methods used by trainers and practitioners reflect this general lack of agreement. Many of the tests for measuring EI are useful to a degree in making people more aware of the issues involved and suggesting where their emotional strengths and weaknesses may lie.

A further problem is that research suggests that successful people with high EI also have high cognitive analytical skills, so there is some indication that the combination of EI and IQ is what makes these people successful.

EI tests usually take the form of questionnaires or psychometric testing, measuring competencies or characteristics such as emotional energy, stress, assertiveness, sociability, attitudes, decisiveness, objective judgement, self-esteem, courage, tolerance and consideration for others. Some tests are web-based; others are paper-based. An example of a basic EI indicator is given at the end of this checklist.

As a manager you should avoid:

- assuming that you or others don't bring emotions to work – feelings can be hidden, but not dropped at will

- thinking that EI is not a relevant aspect of work behaviour

- assuming that your own EI is confirmed, unchanging and needs no further development

- thinking that there are 'wrong' or 'right' emotions – there are not; all emotions are useful tools and indicators of climate and motivations

- failing to understand that emotions are highly context-dependent and are always the product of an interaction and a specific situation
- forgetting that the appropriateness of emotions will differ in differing cultures.

Emotional Intelligence Indicator

Note that this test has not been validated in any way. It is intended to give a rudimentary illustration of a few of the many characteristics that can make up the overall concept of EI and how they can be assessed to provide indicators for development.

Mark **x** in the appropriate column	1 Low	2	3 Medium	4	5 High
Self-awareness					
You are aware of how you are perceived by others	Never		Sometimes		Always
You are aware that your moods can affect others for better or worse	Never		Sometimes		Always
You are confident of your abilities and feel that most people respect you	Rarely		Sometimes		Always
Emotional resilience					
You are determined to see things through to completion	Not often		Usually		Always
You are comfortable when you have to overrule others' firmly held views	Never		Usually		Always
You are easily depressed if things go wrong	Always		Sometimes		Never
Motivation					
You always look for new challenges and to exceed existing targets	Never		Sometimes		Always

Mark **x** in the appropriate column	1 Low	2	3 Medium	4	5 High
You always encourage your staff to do the same	Never		Sometimes		Always
You find it difficult to exercise self-discipline	Always		Sometimes		Never
Empathy					
You find it hard to be a good listener	Always		Sometimes		Never
You take into account other people's concerns	Never		Sometimes		Always
You sense what other people are feeling without being told	Never		Sometimes		Always
Social skills					
You feel uneasy talking to large groups	Always		Sometimes		Never
You are comfortable when meeting and dealing with new people	Never		Sometimes		Always
You always try to get people to work together, not against each other	Never		Sometimes		Always

Maximum score: 75

Your score:

Daniel Goleman
Emotional intelligence

Introduction

Daniel Goleman is usually credited with challenging the traditional view of IQ (intelligence quotient) by drawing together research on how the brain works and developing this to promote and popularise the concept of emotional intelligence (EI, sometimes referred to as EQ) in a highly accessible form.

In *Working with Emotional Intelligence* (1998), Goleman defined emotional intelligence as a capacity for recognising our own and others' feelings, for motivating ourselves, and for managing our emotions, both within ourselves and in our relationships.

Life and background

Goleman, born in 1946, gained his PhD in psychology from Harvard, where he also taught. His best-selling book, *Emotional Intelligence: Why it Matters more than IQ*, was published in 1995, and in 1998 was followed by *Working with Emotional Intelligence*. Goleman has frequently written for the *New York Times* on behavioural science and is currently the chief executive of Emotional Intelligence Services in Sudbury, Massachusetts, which is affiliated with the Hay Group and offers courses in training and assessment for emotional intelligence. He is also co-chairman of the Rutgers University-based Consortium for Research on Emotional Intelligence and a co-founder of the Collaborative for Academic, Social and Emotional Learning at the Yale University

Child Studies Center (now based at the University of Illinois at Chicago).

Goleman's interest in EI arose from a realisation that a high IQ is not necessarily a prerequisite for having a successful life. In *Emotional Intelligence* he identifies many people who, while brilliant academically, were failures socially or in corporate life. Conversely, he identifies others who were not well qualified or distinguished in academic terms, but were still highly successful in their lives and business achievements. Goleman went on to relate business acumen to emotional intelligence. In *Working with Emotional Intelligence* he identified 25 EI competencies, or surface behaviours, and discussed how high emotional intelligence can make all the difference between success and failure.

Principal theories

Emotional intelligence and the brain

In *Emotional Intelligence*, Goleman describes how the evolution of the brain has implications for our emotions and behavioural responses. He outlines how, during its evolution over millions of years, the brain has come to comprise three main areas:

- **Brain stem** – situated at the base of the brain and at the top of the spinal cord. It controls bodily functions and instinctive survival responses, and is the most primitive part of the brain.

- **Hippocampus** – evolved after the brain stem and is situated just above it. It includes the amygdala region, the importance of which was identified by Joseph LeDoux during the 1980s. Here, the brain stores emotional, survival-linked responses to visual and other inputs. The amygdala seems able to hijack the brain in some circumstances, taking over people's reactions literally before they have had time to think, and provoking an immediate response to a situation. Mammals or human beings who have had their amygdala removed show no signs of emotional feeling. The amygdala can catalyse the sort of impulsive actions that may sometimes overpower rational thought and the capacity for considered reactions.

● **Neocortex** – the large, well-developed, top region of the brain which comprises the centre for our thinking, memory and reasoning functions.

Through evolution, our emotions and thinking intelligence – the two main functions of the brain regulating our behaviour – are situated in separate areas. Furthermore, our emotional centres receive input before our thinking centres, and can react quickly and strongly in some situations. The results of this for human behaviour can be catastrophic. If we are not aware of the situation and practised in controlling our initial feelings, we may allow inappropriate emotional responses to pre-empt behaviour based on consideration of more appropriate options. Our emotions have a wisdom of their own that we should learn to use more, particularly in terms of the intuitive sense they offer. Yet when people first confront stimuli that prompt, for example, extreme fear, anger, or frustration, their first impulse to active response comes from the amygdala. If intelligent control is not exerted, the brain moves into survival mode, stimulating instinctive actions that, while possibly right for the situation, are not rationally considered and may be wrong.

Today, we usually have no need to fight or run away from dangers of the sort faced by people in prehistoric times. While some instinctive reactions may be wise in some circumstances, we need to be aware of how the primitive response in the brain's emotional centre precedes all rational evaluation and response. Emotional intelligence involves controlling our instinctive responses to take account of this.

Goleman's framework of emotional intelligence

Goleman developed a framework to explain EI in terms of five elements he described as self-awareness, self-regulation, motivation, empathy and social skills. Each of these elements has distinctive characteristics:

- **Self-awareness** – examining how your emotions affect your performance; using your values to guide decision-making; self-assessment – looking at your strengths and weaknesses and learning from your experiences; and being self-confident and certain about your capabilities, values and goals.

- **Self-regulation** – controlling your temper; controlling your stress by being more positive and action-centred; retaining composure and the ability to think clearly under pressure; handling impulses well; and nurturing trustworthiness and self-restraint.

- **Motivation** – enjoying challenge and stimulation; seeking out achievement; commitment; ability to take the initiative; optimism; and being guided by personal preferences in choosing goals.

- **Empathy** – the ability to see other people's points of view; behaving openly and honestly; avoiding the tendency to stereotype others; and being culturally aware.

- **Social skills** – the use of influencing skills such as persuasion; good communication with others, including employees; listening skills; negotiation; cooperation; dispute resolution; ability to inspire and lead others; capacity to initiate and manage change; and ability to deal with others' emotions – particularly group emotions.

Goleman claims that people who demonstrate these characteristics are more likely to be successful in senior management, citing research from various sources that suggests senior managers with a higher emotional intelligence rating perform better than those without. He gives several anecdotal case studies to illustrate ways in which EI can make a real impact in the workplace.

The Emotional Competence Inventory

Goleman believes that emotional intelligence can be developed over a period of time. He devised an Emotional Competence Inventory (ECI), in association with the Hay Group, to use in assessing and developing EI competencies at work. The ECI reduces the original five components of EI to four:

1 Self-awareness
- being aware of your emotions and their significance
- having a realistic knowledge of your strengths and weaknesses
- having confidence in yourself and your capacities.

2 Self-management
- controlling your emotions
- being honest and trustworthy
- being flexible and dedicated.

3 Social competence
- being empathic, being able to perceive another's thoughts and points of view
- being aware of and sensing a group's dynamics and interrelationships
- focusing on others' needs, particularly when they are customers.

4 Social skills
- helping others to develop themselves
- effective leadership
- influencing skills
- excellent interpersonal communication skills
- change-management skills
- ability to resolve arguments and discord
- ability to nourish and build good relationships
- team-player skills.

Goleman, in association with Hay McBer, has more recently been involved in researching leadership styles, as he reported in a

2000 *Harvard Business Review* article. The research, in which 3,781 executive participants took part, suggests that leaders gain the best results by using a combination of six leadership styles, each of which has a central characteristic feature and uses different components of emotional intelligence:

- **Coercive leaders** demand instant obedience. They are self-motivated, initiate change and are driven to succeed.
- **Authoritative leaders** energise people towards a goal. They initiate change and are empathic.
- **Affiliative leaders** build relationships. They are empathic and have good communication skills.
- **Democratic leaders** actively encourage team involvement in decision-making. They are good at communication, listening and negotiation.
- **Pacesetting leaders** set high standards of performance. They use their initiative and are self-motivated and driven to succeed.
- **Coaching leaders** expand and develop people's skills. They have the abilities to listen well, communicate effectively and motivate others.

The research findings suggest that the six leadership styles are each appropriate for different types of situations, and that leadership styles have a direct influence on the working atmosphere of an organisation; this, in turn, influences financial results.

Primal leadership (2002), written by Goleman with co-authors Richard Boyatzis and Annie McKee, explores the role of emotional intelligence in leadership and in particular how a leader's positive or negative emotions can affect an organisation.

In perspective

The conviction that success depends to a high degree on interpersonal skills is not new, and Goleman has often been criticised for taking others' ideas, to some extent, and repackaging them as a new concept. Goleman, however, freely discusses the origins of his ideas, and acknowledges fellow academics when he uses their work.

In critical article in 2001 Charles Woodruffe, reviewing Goleman's version of EI, suggested that:

- Goleman contradicts himself in claiming that emotional intelligence is inherent and biologically based, yet is a skill that can be learned and developed

- the self-report measures of emotional intelligence used by Goleman have considerable limitations, particularly in terms of accuracy

- the EI behaviours or competencies put forward by Goleman, such as self-confidence and leadership, are not at all new, and are factors that have often been recognised as commonly associated with high achievement levels.

Whatever truth there might be in these criticisms, Goleman has certainly promoted management thinking on the subject of EI. He has taken some complex ideas relating to human behaviour and biological evolution and expressed them in a simpler and more comprehensible form which, under the label 'emotional intelligence', is easy to understand. As a result, many people have found his core proposition, that we can use intelligence to better manage our emotions and draw on our emotional intuition to guide our thinking, to be a helpful approach in both their lives and their work.

Marketing yourself

Marketing theory focuses an organisation's or individual's attention on the perceived needs and wants of the marketplace. Philip Kotler has defined marketing as a human activity directed at satisfying needs and wants through exchange processes.

For the purposes of this checklist the exchange processes comprise skills, techniques, abilities, competence and image, and they take place between (potential) employer and employee, or between customer and supplier.

The idea of 'marketing yourself' is challenging for some, but most of us recognise that the way others see us has a major impact on our professional life and that it is vital to give attention to the way we present ourselves to others such as colleagues, clients, potential business partners and prospective employers. Like it or not, you are always selling yourself, whether you are looking for a new job, negotiating a deal or pursuing a business opportunity.

Whatever you are selling – cars, perfume or your own skills and talents – to an employer or customer, the principles of sales and marketing are the same. It is no good being strong, confident and skilled if you keep it a secret. You must know your strengths and focus on them, and at the same time know your weaknesses and minimise them. To be successful, you will have to let the rest of the world know about yourself. This checklist applies the principles of sales and marketing at an individual level to help you present yourself to the best advantage.

Successfully marketing yourself involves:

- taking a positive attitude
- knowing what you want
- self-confidence – believing in yourself
- increasing your visibility
- reviewing your image
- being enthusiastic and passionate about your work
- seeking professional help and advice where necessary
- networking as much as possible
- making the most of opportunities
- capitalising on your strengths and making them work for you
- using online media tools including social media.

Action checklist

1 Familiarise yourself with the product

Marketing yourself starts with knowing yourself.

You need to know:

- what the product is
- what its strengths and weaknesses are
- what opportunities and threats there are
- what image the package is projecting
- who the product is directed at
- who is going to buy it
- what is changing around you, and how to react to this innovation.

Look at yourself objectively to identify your skills and qualities. Try to see yourself as if you were an external observer. Watch yourself entering a room; think of the impression you make and what you would want to change.

2 Be aware of the product's inherent strengths and weaknesses

Bear in mind that there are three 'yous': who you really are, what you want to be, and what people think you are. Make sure you know all of three.

Consider:

- how well you can motivate and negotiate
- how well you manage time and keep your promises to others
- how well you cope under pressure
- how often you put off difficult tasks
- how effective you are working on your own or as part of a team
- how flexible and adaptable you are to new challenges and what kind of reaction you will have to forthcoming changes
- how you learn best, and least well – do you like to get on with things, try them and learn as you go, or do you prefer to hold back, reflect and think things through before getting involved?
- whether you are at the peak, the trough or in the middle of a learning curve, whether you know what you want to tackle next, or whether you have plateaued – albeit temporarily
- how authentic you appear – be yourself, as others will soon realise if you are playing a part.

You may find it helpful at this point to undertake some form of personal assessment, such as the Myers-Briggs Type Indicator.

3 List product features and benefits

People often describe themselves solely in terms of what they are. Talking in terms of benefits means focusing on how your characteristics will benefit the customer/employer. For example, a willingness to take on responsibility (feature) implies capability to accept more delegated tasks (benefit to employer).

Feature	Benefit
Punctual, reliable	Consistency
Delivers on time	Trustworthiness
Diligent, productive	Cost-effectiveness
Ambitious	Drive and energy

4 Be aware of product stereotypes

Some jobs are characterised by high turnover (retail, publishing), others as universally 'solid' (accounting, teaching); some as exciting and attractive (media, travel), others as intellectual and 'clever' (lecturing, journalism). However wrong the stereotype in reality, bear in mind that people's traditional perceptions will influence their perception of you. Make sure that, if necessary, you act in such a way as to challenge that stereotype so that people know who you really are.

5 Ensure the quality of the product

To improve product quality, you must learn from your mistakes. Learning to do this is an important part of quality and marketing processes. It helps you to build confidence in yourself and, in turn, others will have confidence in you. Self-confidence is a necessary prerequisite to self-marketing, although excessive confidence can be a turn-off. The contrary is also true: when you don't believe in yourself, you are only selling yourself short.

6 Work on product image

You have an image whether you like it or not, so you might as well make the best of it. Think of yourself as a brand, a product in the marketplace. As you go through a working day, remember that everything you do, say and write, adds value to – or takes value from – your own 'brand' image.

Recognise that the way you interact with people probably varies from individual to individual; ask yourself what leaves you and them satisfied or dissatisfied, confused or focused. Remember that too much self-deprecation can be as negative as too much self-importance. Focus on the positive – all of us have weaknesses, but we can work to minimise them.

7 Review product packaging

Whenever you can, use good design to present to the world the image that will do the most for you. This does not mean turning yourself into a film star; rather, work at things that improve your image and come reasonably easily to you. It may be your notepaper, business card, the way you present a report, how you communicate to groups, the layout of your office, or even just the way you dress. Think about the norms in the market you wish to succeed in, whether they are formal and traditional or edgy and modern.

Before you leave for work tomorrow take a look in the mirror and ask yourself what your clothes tell other people about you. You can be sure that your clothes convey some kind of image, intended or not, so at least be aware of it. Decide whether you want to do anything about it. Remember that more than half the image you create is in the way you look. First impressions are important, as it can be difficult to change what people think about you later on, no matter how inaccurate their initial impression may have been.

Your voice is as important as the way you look, and its tone, inflection and accent can inspire confidence – or the opposite – without your knowing or intending it. What mood does your voice convey? Are there things you want to change? It's not so much what you say but the way that you say it that counts.

Watch your body language: how you walk, whether you constantly fidget with your hands, whether you frown a lot, whether you look directly at people when you talk to them. Learn to relax when the going gets tough – it gives the impression that you are on top of the situation.

Consult friends as to how you are coming across; the odds are that you will be surprised. Remember it is impossible for us to see ourselves as others see us. If your self-image is badly in conflict with the image others have of you, efforts to market yourself may end in disaster.

8 Create product awareness

Get yourself, your name and your face known. This can be achieved in many ways, for example, by:

- extending your contacts
- getting involved
- organising
- writing articles
- doing voluntary or charity work
- getting involved in professional bodies, for example as a committee member
- speaking up at meetings
- volunteering new ideas
- taking risks
- finding a mentor
- writing and commenting on blogs
- believing in yourself
- being memorable – as long as it is in a positive way.

Be aware too that it is possible to overcook the goose – too much exposure is as dangerous as not enough.

9 Promote the product

Make a list of the people or categories of people who need to know about you so that you can further exploit your skills, increase the profitability of your business, or make the next move in your career.

Accurate targeting is a crucial ingredient of marketing and is more rewarding than the scattergun shot-in-the-dark approach. Give yourself the best chances you can by identifying the profile of your best customer.

Be aware of the importance of influencing others in a positive way. In his book *Influence: The Psychology of Persuasion*, Robert Cialdini describes six principles of influence: authority, consistency, reciprocation, social proof (finding out what other people are doing), scarcity and liking. Think about the benefits of applying these principles; for example, if you are consistent, you are likely to be viewed by others as being both authentic and reliable.

10 Take advantage of opportunities to promote the product virtually

Nowadays, employers and other contacts are likely to look for information about you online. Try putting your name into an internet search engine and see what the top results are. You may or may not be happy with the results but by being proactive on the web you will be able to influence what people know about you and how they perceive you. However, there are risks involved with an online presence, so do consider:

- how to reflect your personality while still maintaining a professional image
- what information you wish to share
- how much time you wish to devote to virtual tools
- which channels to use, for example a blog, Twitter or LinkedIn
- what messages you want to send out about yourself
- using privacy settings appropriately.

Although web networking has many benefits, remember that it will work best when supported by face-to-face networking and interactions.

11 Set product targets

Sometimes we can be reluctant to set challenging goals because they seem distant and unreachable. Break daunting processes down into small, achievable steps. Make them SMART (specific, measurable, attainable, realistic and timely). Don't think of yourself as starting from point A and magically arriving at point Z; instead envisage yourself going through each step, concentrating on getting the detail right, learning from mistakes and enjoying the fact that you are making progress. Always remind yourself what the objectives are and do not forget to celebrate the short-term wins.

As a manager you should avoid:

- being afraid to make changes
- being negative about yourself
- being excessively modest about your achievements
- hiding yourself away
- ignoring the value of personal contacts.

Leading from the middle

There is no commonly agreed definition for leadership, but a suggested one is the capacity to establish direction, to influence and align others towards a common aim, to motivate and commit them to action, and to encourage them to feel responsible for their performance.

Leadership is often seen as the key to improved performance. It is needed at all levels in an organisation, not just the top. Think about situations you have observed – you may recall people who were at the bottom of the hierarchy, or in positions with no formal authority, but were still able to provide a lead for others.

Many businesses adopt a matrix approach to organisation, and individual managers may need to lead a diverse team from several parts of an organisation. For larger organisations spread throughout a number of countries, team members may rarely or never meet face-to-face, and so will need to lead virtual or remote teams. In these types of teams, particularly, leadership is vital for delivering products or services.

Most people would agree that leadership can be developed, and that there are some definable leadership skills that can help managers to get the most from their team. Many organisations now run programmes to improve the leadership skills of employees at all levels from supervisor through to managing director. This checklist seeks to explain the fundamentals of leadership, taking leaders as people who:

● make followers feel well supported, and can be trusted and relied upon by team members

● have a clear, exciting image of the future and can lead the way through change

● show commitment to, and generate enthusiasm for, the organisation

● are honest and open and spend time talking and listening to their people

● give employees the room and the confidence to get their job done.

Action checklist

1 Be clear about the difference between management and leadership

There is some disagreement about the differences between management and leadership. Some experts, such as Henry Mintzberg, think that it is difficult and unhelpful to separate them; others think they should be clearly distinguished. Most would agree, however, that managers and supervisors need some leadership ability. Definitions of both areas and their argued differences vary, so you need to be clear and think out your own approach to the subject before you can work to improve your leadership skills. A common approach to the difference is that:

● management is about the day-to-day running of a function and getting the right people in the right place, with a focus on implementation

● leadership is about creating a vision for that function and gaining people's commitment by providing strategic direction.

2 Be clear about where you are now

Are you comfortable with the idea of being a leader? If not, where do you think your weaknesses lie? Many people – especially those who have been promoted because they have a technical skill – feel uncomfortable about leadership. Think about yourself as a leader and consider whether you feel that leadership is alien to your character, that you may lack the authority and respect to be a leader, or that it is only more senior managers who should be leaders.

Remember that everyone can learn how to develop their leadership potential – authority and respect are there to be earned. Today, people at all levels are expected to show leadership qualities.

3 Downplay charisma

Charisma used to be seen as the key to a leader's success. But most experts today do not take its existence seriously and it is viewed as something of a blunt weapon. The trouble with relying on charisma is that it can be destructive, and it tends to dominate people. Organisations need empowered people who can make their own decisions, not slavish followers who look to a leader for guidance and direction at every turn. Rather than allowing a leadership cult to develop, or relying on personality or charismatic appeal, a range of leadership skills and styles needs to be developed for successful leadership.

4 Recognise the different leadership needs of people

You should work at developing a range of leadership styles and matching your leadership style to the situation and the people. Different people will need different kinds of leadership:

- people who fail to take responsibility need a directional style – give strict targets and ensure that these are monitored

- employees who lack confidence, but show potential, will benefit from a coaching approach – be directive and supportive and explain what needs to be done, but reinforce their positive behaviour and get them to take responsibility

- talented but underachieving employees should be led through communication – help them to perform better through involving them in decision-making and supporting them in taking the initiative

- star performers who are already fully competent need to be appreciated – leave them alone to get on with the job.

  Situational leadership theory is a good basis for understanding the need to work at acquiring different leadership styles. The theory is that the 'best' leadership approaches are relative to specific contexts and situations rather than as attributes of particular personalities. R. H. Hall's emergent leader approach (1972) is one example; another is Ken Blanchard and Paul Hersey's well-known situational leadership theory, developed in 1982.

5 Build up a range of demonstrable leadership attributes that confirm you as a leader in the eyes of your people

Demonstrable leadership attributes that will help you to lead others include:

- developing and demonstrating good work habits
- understanding and valuing the work of your people
- handling pressure effectively
- clearly demonstrating the values you hold
- encouraging the enthusiasm of your team
- providing regular feedback
- listening and learning.

6 Build communication channels

Develop the right mix of communication, so that people get to know what you expect, can understand if they have done well or badly, and feel that they are able to give you feedback on your own performance.

Most research into what makes a good leader stresses that leaders communicate all the time. They create a vision of where the department and organisation are going, and they do so by communicating it clearly and often, demonstrating it through actions and listening to their people.

7　Work hard at empowering your staff

You need to provide the support and develop the confidence that will help team members achieve things for themselves. Today's leaders work at creating the right environment and circumstances so that people can take ownership of their work. Are you courageous enough to trust your people to do a good job, and to show faith in them? If you are, and can still give them a sense of vision and guidance when they need it, they will see you as their leader.

As a manager you should avoid:

- behaving in a domineering way
- thinking that leaders have to come up with all the ideas – or are the only ones who have ideas
- relying on charisma
- refusing to listen to your people.

Managing (your relationship with) your boss

Managing your boss is about developing a relationship of trust, respect and mutual support, which enables you to perform well within your job role and to develop your skills, knowledge and career. It means acknowledging who is the boss but retaining the ability to do the best you can for the organisation, the team and yourself. A good working relationship between a manager and his or her boss should involve fairness, mutual respect, trust and rapport as well as open and honest communication. The key word is 'manage', implying an ongoing process rather than a one-off activity.

The relationship you have with your boss plays a fundamental role in your ability to do your job well. In fact your relationship with your boss is the most important workplace relationship you have. Putting effort into building a productive and communicative working relationship with your boss ensures that you both know what is feasible and possible, and contributes to achieving the results that matter to you both. Good working relationships improve self-esteem, aid your personal development and put you in a strong position to overcome any problems or conflicts that may arise.

The relationship between manager and boss needs to be actively managed. It is not just a case of being pleasant or getting along well together – what is being managed is the relationship, not the individual.

It is important to take the time and trouble to talk to each other. This will help you form an alliance and work together towards common goals. It will also give you a better understanding of your manager's objectives and values. This in turn will enable you to support your manager in his or her weaker areas. However, be wary of encouraging your boss to think that an idea you contributed was actually theirs.

This checklist will help those who wish, or need, to manage the relationship with their boss more effectively. Remember to appraise and review your current work, future goals and the interaction you have with your manager at regular intervals to ensure that a good working relationship is maintained.

Action checklist

1 Communicate clearly

Prevention is better than cure, and effective communication prevents a lot of misunderstandings and breakdowns in relationships. Make sure that you share information in a timely way, regularly and in adequate detail. Pay attention to formal communication, but also ensure you simply talk and compare notes from time to time. Don't be afraid of asking for help if you need it.

2 Identify any blockages

Think about what may be blocking the way to a good working relationship. Consider your boss's behaviour and personal characteristics. Both can have a significant bearing on the development and quality of your relationship. Also be mindful that your behaviour will influence how your boss behaves towards you too. Leader-member exchange (LMX) theory supports this notion, arguing that a person's perception of their boss may be at odds with how other members of the team perceive their leader. In a similar way, your boss may behave differently with your colleagues than with you. When evaluating the relationship, do so within the context of how well or badly others get on with your boss. This will help you identify whether it is your behaviour

or attitude that may be adversely affecting the quality of your
relationship.

There may be other 'blockages' to a good working relationship –
you may have trouble communicating, or find it hard to express
your opinions or discuss workload issues. Identify what triggers
these problems, being honest about your own weaknesses. Also
consider which aspects of the relationship work well. Build upon
these and work on reducing problems in other areas.

3 Identify your boss's leadership style

The way in which your boss acts or behaves towards you can
also be affected by their leadership style, be it transactional or
transformational. Your boss may take a bureaucratic, charismatic,
dictatorial, consultative, or laissez-faire approach to leadership,
any of which can affect your relationship with them. A specific
style or mix of styles will require different approaches from you.
Consider also your boss's 'thinking' style. It's no surprise that
we get on well with some people, especially those who think like
us, but others can easily rub us up the wrong way. Try to figure
out whether your boss focuses on minutiae or the 'big picture',
is reactive or proactive, likes or hates change, is a right-brain or
left-brain person.

4 Identify your boss's objectives and values

Think about what is important to your boss and work hard on
these areas. The two main areas to pay attention to are:

- what, in the eyes of your manager, the key objectives are and
what support you can give towards achieving them

- what personal values your boss holds dear, such as customer
care. Work on supporting these values and don't do things that
are contrary to them.

You should also consider your boss's motives and personal
ambitions, such as promotions and achievements they want to
gain for themselves. Think about where your boss has come
from in terms of former employment, educational background

and so on. How much is your boss interested in the organisation compared with his or her own career development? Be wary of evidently self-interested values, such as personal status. Having an understanding of such matters will help you to understand their motives and their approach to managing you.

5 Clarify boundaries of responsibility

Sort out with your boss exactly what decisions you can make:

- after discussion with your boss
- on your own but reporting to your boss afterwards
- on your own with no need to report.

Lack of clarity can be a major source of conflict and friction. If you are clear about your sphere of responsibility, you will gain confidence in decision-making and avoid the need to keep referring small matters to your boss. Constant pestering runs the risk of irritating the boss and giving the impression that you lack confidence in your job.

6 Tackle the simple issues

Look through the problems you have identified and decide which will be easy to resolve. Can small administrative problems be addressed by simply introducing a new system? Discuss minor sensitivities (such as opening the office window, working in silence or with background noise) with your boss and try to reach a compromise. Don't waste time reporting minor successes.

Work overload is a common cause of conflict. Don't take on work you can't manage – be honest, but remember your boss's objectives and always suggest an alternative solution. Don't underestimate yourself or your point of view. If you don't have faith in your ability to do a good job and develop in your role, your boss certainly won't.

7 Tackle longer-term issues with assertiveness

Some blockages cannot be dealt with overnight. Concentrate on building a stronger relationship with your boss over the long term. This means being assertive but not aggressive. Express your point of view, respect your boss's opinions and work to find mutually acceptable solutions to existing problems. This will improve your relationship and help you handle difficult situations more effectively in the future. Resolve not to go over your boss's head, however attractive this may seem. If you feel blocked, tackle the issues directly to avoid creating more problems later.

8 Focus on loyalty and support

Focus on supporting your boss in any weak areas they may have, without making it too obvious that you are doing so. Find out which parts of the business they enjoy and are good at, and which they don't like doing or perhaps don't have the skills to deal with. Make yourself indispensable. Show you are keen to learn skills that complement your boss's skills. Win their trust by achieving things they value. Together you can become a winning team.

9 Think about how others see you

People make big assumptions about your abilities from the way you look or the way you present yourself. They may assume that a scruffy, untidy looking person is disorganised, bad at their job and generally unreliable. Look smart. Smile and demonstrate a positive approach. Celebrate your successes. Make sure that your manager knows when you have done well and understand that your success reflects on them too.

10 Take advantage of opportunities that present themselves

Keep your eye on the big picture and not just the task in hand. Don't use work overload as an excuse to avoid activities such as attending conferences or meeting senior directors. Weigh up the short-term disadvantages against the potential longer-term value to the organisation. Think about what these opportunities could contribute to your development and what you could learn from them.

11 Communicate your own agenda

There's no need to be abrasive, but a modicum of repetition may be useful in making sure that your ideas are heard. This may relate to specific projects or ongoing work, but think about the bigger picture too. What do you want to learn? Where do you want your career to go? Instead of always playing your boss's tune, develop joint objectives.

12 Review issues and actions, and plan future development

Review issues which are important to you and discuss them with your boss. They should matter to your boss because if you fail, so will your boss. Discuss problems before they get out of hand and have some ideas for solutions ready for discussion.

13 When relationships are genuinely difficult

Most of this checklist is valid if you have a boss who acts reasonably. Sometimes you may be faced with a difficult boss. Three of the worst types are the bully, the sexually harassing boss and the glory-stealing boss. It is not easy to deal with any of these, although employment law does provide some protection in respect of the first two. Techniques such as keeping records, collecting evidence and bypassing your boss can be useful to deal with the glory-stealer.

14 Nip conflict in the bud

If conflict breaks out between you and your boss, handle it. Don't run away or tackle anger with anger.

15 Review the relationship

Sit down from time to time and ask yourself: 'How are we doing?' Make an assessment of your interactions, so that you both know how things stand, and can work to improve and maintain the underlying relationship. Use instances of success or failure as a vehicle for reviewing the relationship. Work out what to repeat in the future and what to do differently next time.

As a manager you should avoid:

- being passive – never questioning what your boss wants and failing to put forward personal viewpoints
- being aggressive – fighting fire with fire rarely works
- going over your boss's head if it can possibly be avoided
- ignoring problems and avoiding any discussion of them
- blaming your boss for 'blockages' in the relationship without also looking at your own behaviour
- failing to communicate openly.

Preparing for a performance appraisal

A performance appraisal is a face-to-face discussion on job performance and objectives between an employee and another person, usually their line manager. A set framework is used as a basis for reviewing and appraising the employee's past performance; providing guidance for improvements; discussing needs and opportunities for learning and development; reaching mutual agreement on objectives and targets for the future.

Performance appraisals, meetings or reviews, or progress meetings as they are now sometimes called, provide a regular opportunity for line managers and employees to review the employee's performance in their job and discuss work objectives for the future. In recent years the focus of performance appraisals has shifted from simple evaluation to performance improvement and development. Performance appraisal is no longer regarded as an annual opportunity for the line manager to give an assessment of performance. It normally takes place within the framework of an overall organisational performance management system. Six-monthly reviews and regular one-to-one meetings give both line managers and employees opportunities to raise issues of concern as they arise throughout the year. The annual performance meeting should not lead line managers to neglect their day-to-day management responsibilities so that issues raised with employees at an appraisal come as a surprise; and employees should not have to wait for an annual meeting to raise any concerns they have relating to their work.

The appraisal meeting should involve an open and honest discussion with a focus on evidence of performance rather than personal opinions. The discussion should be guided by an emphasis on performance improvement and development, covering any issues and problems; it should also support the employee's personal growth. It is important to consider the impact of past and forthcoming changes in the workplace, looking at whether goals and objectives need to be amended or development activities planned. This checklist provides guidance for employees preparing for a performance appraisal. They should expect to:

- get advance notice of the appraisal and sufficient time to prepare
- be given a clear picture of what to expect at the appraisal
- be given enough time for the appraisal itself, such as one hour, in a suitable private location
- receive the undivided and uninterrupted attention of the line manager
- be able to discuss priorities
- receive feedback on performance
- know what the feedback is based on and who has given the feedback (for example, 360 degree, supervisor, etc)
- be heard and respected
- be offered constructive guidance on attaining agreed goals
- receive help with personal development plans and targets
- take responsibility for their own performance
- understand how their work relates to both team and organisational objectives
- have the opportunity to discuss how organisational changes will affect their work.

Action checklist

1 Understand the objectives and terms of reference

Appraisals are usually part of an overall scheme of performance management and follow an established framework set by your employer or manager. Make sure that you understand how the scheme works. For a successful appraisal, you need:

- a clear understanding of the purpose and the process of the appraisal

- a clear understanding of the terms of reference of the appraisal – whether it is linked to pay, what evaluation criteria are used and how they are applied

- thorough preparation by both employee and line manager

- a resolve to tackle problems honestly

- a relaxed attitude, even if past objectives have not been achieved

- a positive approach, especially in terms of further personal development

- time and an appropriate location for the appraisal.

2 Agree a date for the appraisal

Ideally, at least two weeks should be allowed for preparation and reflection, so the date should be agreed a few weeks before the meeting takes place to give you reasonable time to prepare.

3 Prepare for the meeting

You and your manager should be provided with a template form or guidance notes on the purpose of the appraisal and an outline of the structure of the meeting. This will help both of you prepare and for the appraisee to consider what evidence they can show to support their achievements. Broadly, appraisals will be in two sections: reviewing the past year's performance and agreeing goals and objectives for the next year.

4 The appraisal itself

Although your manager will lead the appraisal, you will be expected to contribute substantially to the discussion. Areas to focus on include:

- tasks or projects that gave you particular satisfaction, and why
- tasks or projects that gave you least satisfaction, and why
- your overall performance
- challenges you face and difficulties you foresee
- areas for improvement
- objectives for the coming year
- short- and long-term personal development needs.

5 Ask for, and give, feedback

You should be given feedback on your work performance and contribution. You should also offer your own feedback to your manager, using events, instances and examples to highlight aspects of learning and development.

6 Don't be reticent about problems

Use the appraisal to discuss any issues or problems that may be affecting your performance. For example, a faulty piece of equipment may be delaying your efforts, you may have to attend lots of meetings, or you may feel you need extra help. Whatever the issues involved, open discussion is essential to resolving problems and you can propose your own solutions.

7 Establish priorities

You and your manager may have differing views on what your priorities should be. There may be reasons for your differing perspectives: for example, your manager may be trying to align the department's output with organisational goals and objectives, while your focus may be on balancing different priorities, work structure problems or time limitations. Discussion should help to clarify the issues so that you can both arrive at an agreed set of priorities.

8 Bring departmental relationships into the open

Discuss any difficulties or problems you have experienced with other people or departments, especially if these have not been discussed before or past discussions have failed to resolve the issues. You need to give clear examples of how you are being affected and consider what suggestions you can make to help improve working relationships.

9 Propose objectives

Do not go into an appraisal meeting assuming that your manager will have your next set of goals and targets finely defined. Work out your own proposals, your own tactics and your own targets, and remember that you have an advantage your manager should recognise, in that you are the one who is doing the job.

10 Agree goals and targets

The setting of goals and targets should not be a one-way process. If changes are needed, these can be discussed. At best, you can discuss with your manager a reassessment of factors contributing to the need for change. Don't be afraid to take a completely fresh look – you may need to establish different kinds of goals and targets, or consider other ways of achieving business and personal development objectives. Make sure that objectives are SMART (specific, measurable, achievable, realistic and timely). This will help both you and your line manager monitor progress accurately and assess the extent to which they have been achieved.

11 Agree further learning and development plans

As well as specific problems and concerns, discuss aspects of continuing development which have not yet been addressed or which form part of a general programme of skills acquisition. Make time to reflect on and plan a flexible development programme that will benefit both you and your work.

12 Explain personal development requirements

Your manager will help you identify training or development needs. Take the opportunity to review your competence and capabilities, both technically and in terms of general management development. Think about your potential future development and promotion opportunities, as well as your immediate job. Consider, for example, what you would like to be doing in, say, three years' time.

13 Identify the support required

Once objectives have been agreed and targets set, assess whether you need extra support to move forward, such as training, resources, or even time for further clarification.

14 Agree the evaluation

If the appraisal has an evaluation element rather than the discussion focus that this checklist assumes, be clear about what you can contribute to the process and how far you agree with the overall evaluation.

15 Do the summing-up

The appraiser will usually summarise agreed action points and plans from the discussion. It is important that you 'own' the tasks and activities ahead and that these are clarified and expressed in a way that you understand. On receiving the summary, ask about anything that you do not understand, and suggest any changes or adjustments you think are necessary. The summary or report gives both you and your manager a signed record of agreement for the future, and will act as a useful reminder on what you need to do before your next meeting.

You should avoid:

- viewing appraisals as a threat rather than an opportunity
- sidestepping difficult issues

- allowing emotions to take over
- failing to challenge any unfair conclusions or decisions
- being overcritical of other departments or colleagues
- attributing blame for difficulties to the personal characteristics of others.

Participating in projects

A project is a carefully selected set of activities chosen to use resources (time, money, energy, space, provisions, and so on) to meet pre-defined objectives and to support business goals, usually with agreed start and end dates.

For the individual, participating in projects can broaden experience and exposure to other parts of the business, and develop skills in team working, communication, influencing others, project planning and project control. Participation in projects can be stimulating, motivational and developmental. It may ultimately lead to career progression. For the company, encouraging participation in projects will draw on people's critical skills and knowledge (at whatever level in the organisation) and make their work more interesting. Projects foster cross-functional understanding and team working, and drive efficient and effective working in the organisation.

This checklist looks at how managers can be involved in projects and keep up with their regular job.

Action checklist

1 Project prioritisation within organisations

At the organisational level, projects will need to be prioritised in some way. An organisation has limited resources and has to ensure these are devoted to activities that will maximise the return on investment. It is unlikely that all project ideas or activities can be pursued, so it is wise to filter these through an evaluative process. One approach is to set up a proposal and business-case template document that has to be completed for all new project proposals and business cases and submitted for approval before resources are allocated. These can be evaluated together on a regular basis at senior management or board level, perhaps monthly, quarterly, annually or biennially, depending on the size of the organisation.

2 Balancing work priorities

At the individual level, we all have limited time and energy, and need to try to find a way of prioritising projects and other work. Overload can lead to stress, inefficiency, errors, and loss of enthusiasm and motivation, so if necessary be prepared to say 'No' to a project, rather than take it on and fail with the project and/or your work. Review your priorities carefully before you commit to a project, and find out what the project leader will expect of you. Discuss the implications with your boss and the project leader, preferably together. Consider:

- how many days (a week, a month, at a time) you will need to give to the project
- where you will have to be to carry out the project requirements
- how these requirements will impact on your regular activities
- what should happen when (not if) there is a conflict of priorities
- what should happen when (not if) the situation changes
- what additional resources you may be able to call on, if necessary
- whether any regular activities could be postponed or normal standards be allowed to slip
- how frequently the situation will need to be reviewed.

Document your understanding of the project requirements and agreements, then send copies to both your boss and the project leader. This should give you a clear, agreed mandate, even though things will change as the project progresses. At times, you will have to cope as best you can with extra workloads, but do not let this get out of hand. When priorities clash, discuss the conflict and how to resolve it with your boss and project leader.

3 Adjusting and managing time

Discuss with your manager possible ways to adjust routine work, or manage time more effectively. For example:

- delegate some regular responsibilities to someone who might be glad of the development opportunity
- adjust work schedules to give you more disposable time for the project's duration
- be realistic rather than perfectionist – aim for 'good enough' where it will do
- encourage effective project meetings with timed agendas, team status reports and action point minutes
- don't attend meetings where you can add no benefit and will see the minutes
- don't try to read all paperwork in detail – instead, scan all but short or important items
- deal with immediate actions quickly, and plan time to handle the rest
- allocate your toughest items to your most productive time of day
- discourage constant interruptions – instead, set 'interruptible' and 'uninterruptible' periods.

4 Getting involved in projects

A project has many players, including the project sponsor, project leader and project team members. There may also be an intermediate programme manager, if there are a number of linked projects.

Key project management relationships are with the project sponsor, who is accountable for success, and has to 'own' the project, and the project manager, who is responsible for delivery on behalf of the sponsor, and has to be given the necessary authority by the sponsor to exercise his or her responsibilities.

The responsibilities of the project sponsor are to:

- determine the prioritisation of a project
- select and approve the project manager
- gain resources for and commit them to the project, for example people, money, space
- approve the project leader's projected estimates of cost, schedule and scope of work
- approve core team members and provide assistance in securing them
- shield the team from politics and non-value-adding outside influences
- promote issues
- be aware of and report on the project's status
- maintain support for and commitment to the project leader and team.

The responsibilities of the project manager are to:

- negotiate with the project sponsor (and programme manager, if appropriate) the initial scope of work, schedule duration and resource needs
- act as the main focal point for the project
- secure the commitment of team members
- communicate the project goals and requirements to all team members
- address customer needs throughout the project
- lead the team through the planning process
- track project progress and initiate any corrective action to keep the project to plan
- communicate the project's status to the project sponsor, team members and interested customers
- step up issues where necessary

- support the project team.

  The responsibilities of project team members are to:
- be directed by the project leader, and maintain an enthusiastic, positive attitude
- be involved in planning the project, and contributing requirements and information from the department and from customers
- be involved in setting the project team's ground rules and adhering to these
- contribute positive, creative suggestions to team meetings, but understand that these may not always be accepted
- support team decisions
- help other team members
- accept responsibility and take ownership for their activities and decisions
- track their activities and stay on schedule
- keep the project leader informed
- inform the project leader early on of any risks, overspends or project delays.

5 Reap the benefits

You will benefit from being involved in projects alongside your regular work activities as much as your organisation does. But you need to take advantage of the benefits deliberately and consciously. Projects can be enormous learning experiences – consolidate your learning by reflecting regularly on new things you now know or can do, and consider how you can continue to apply that learning in day-to-day activities. Use a continuing professional development scheme to record your activities, learning and reflections.

You can gain the most from project work if you:

- ensure that your boss and your project leader know what you achieve in brief, regular status reports

- share your knowledge by coaching others – it benefits you as well as them
- enhance your visibility by letting others know about the project aims and achievements, for example by giving presentations at departmental meetings
- volunteer for other projects.

As a manager you should avoid:

- agreeing to anything that is impossible
- pushing yourself or others too far, even if you feel energised and excited
- getting so involved that you forget about your normal job
- trying to hide problems relating to either the project or your regular activities.

Networking

Networking involves establishing, developing and maintaining informal and formal business relationships with existing and potential colleagues, customers, clients, suppliers and other contacts. It requires an awareness of the value of relationships to both yourself and others. Personal networks overlap – A and B may be in the same network but each will have contacts in other networks.

Taking an organised and proactive approach to networking has many recognised benefits. It can help to improve and extend relationships, bring you into contact with potential customers and suppliers, and build links that will help you in your business and your career. Networking may give you access to important sources of information or be a source of development opportunities, support and influence.

These benefits depend on your investment of time and energy in attending events, keeping in touch with others, and contributing to their interests where possible. Many are happy to do this as a natural part of their personal and working lives, but others find it challenging and will need to put more conscious effort into developing their personal networking skills and extending their personal range of contacts. Networks are not static – they can evolve, expand or shrink depending on the perceived needs and actions of the networker.

For some, the term 'networking' implies an element of manipulation. This need not be the case; networking is a long-established means of building and maintaining business relationships.

There are three types of networks – personal, professional and organisational – but you may find it difficult to distinguish between them, particularly online. This checklist focuses on personal and professional networking.

Action checklist

1 Choose a personal approach to networking

How will you go about networking? What style or approach suits you best? Consider these three styles:

- **Conscious networkers** have clear-cut goals. They recognise what is missing in their networks. They identify those who will meet their needs and make contact and develop relationships with them. These networkers have a considered and systematic approach.

- **Open networkers** also have a considered approach but take a longer-term view, building networks with the future in mind. Their objectives may be less clear-cut than those of intuitive networkers, but they recognise those who may be useful in the future and cultivate relationships with them.

- **Intuitive networkers** are neither systematic nor considered in their approach. They enjoy mixing with people and do so as a matter of course. They may even be unaware of the extent of their range of contacts or of their potential value in a business context.

2 Prepare a brief summary of your business

Prepare a clean, short introductory statement that describes you and your business. If it is longer than a few sentences, you may lose the listener's attention. Adapt the statement to the person you are talking to – this will prevent it sounding too slick. Use humour if you feel people will be comfortable with it. This can create a more relaxed atmosphere and encourage others to join in the conversation. Keep it brief – no one wants to listen to a long diatribe about how wonderful your business is. Let the facts speak for themselves. In some contexts, it can be helpful to have prepared a one- or two-minute presentation on your business.

3 Design your publicity material

Design your business card, and any other literature you produce, to project a professional image of yourself and your business. Take into consideration the factors – colour, logo, layout, message – that will attract attention and make it easy for people to remember you. A business card has two sides: consider listing your services on the reverse. If you are in the import/export business, carry bilingual or multilingual cards; this will make it easier for your foreign customers and suppliers to network with you.

If you produce a brochure, make sure that it is written in plain English, free from jargon. Clear statements with plenty of white space are more effective than cluttered text with excessive use of colour. Communicate in a simple and straightforward manner that you care about your customers and wish to meet their needs, rather than making a high-pressure sales pitch.

4 Attend meetings and events

Exhibitions, trade fairs, seminars, workshops and events organised by Chambers of Commerce, local enterprise networks, business organisations or professional associations all offer opportunities for networking. Don't overload your diary by accepting every invitation, but think about the kind of people you want to meet and which events will give you the best chance of doing so.

5 Make the most of meetings and events

- Arrive in good time: this will give you the best chance of managing the event to your advantage.
- If there is an opportunity to display your brochures, set out a few for people to pick up.

- If name badges are available, wear one. Having your own can be useful, as event badges often use small print. Place your badge high on the right shoulder, so that people will see it easily when shaking hands with you.

- If there is a list of attendees, take a quick look through to identify people you are interested in meeting and keep an eye out for them during the event.

- Don't be afraid to walk up to a small group of people and introduce yourself, but don't monopolise the conversation. Let others do the talking to begin with – this will enable you to learn about them, and what interests and concerns them.

- This is also important when you are introduced to people. Encourage them to talk about their business and their future plans. This information will help you decide how to develop the relationship.

- Think about how long you want to stay with each person. Offer your business card and suggest you might talk again later. Keep the business cards you receive in a different place from your own, or you may find yourself handing out someone else's card.

6 Consider joining a networking group

Professional associations, business clubs and local groups set up specifically for the purpose of networking offer many opportunities to meet new people and expand your network of contacts. Think about whether you wish to meet others in your profession or area of expertise or to broaden your range of contacts. Consider also whether a national, regional or local group would be most beneficial. Take membership requirements and costs into account when deciding which group to join. It is normally possible to attend group meetings to assess their suitability before making a final decision. It is also worth bearing in mind that business clubs often offer training in networking skills.

7 Investigate online networking activities

Networking websites fall into two broad categories: business and personal. But the boundaries are becoming blurred because personal sites are often used for commercial advertising and brand-based networking, while you can find a range of discussions on business sites ranging from the trivial to detailed professional issues. LinkedIn is emerging as the main business-networking site. It offers opportunities to link to colleagues, colleagues of colleagues, and colleagues of those colleagues – giving potential access to thousands of people. The site also hosts interest groups and discussion boards where you can not only network but also raise or answer questions about business issues.

Successful sites such as LinkedIn and Facebook have large numbers of users, so they offer better networking opportunities than smaller sites. Some formerly successful sites such as MySpace have fallen from their pre-eminent positions, while other networking facilities such as the virtual world of Second Life have never really fulfilled their potential. Twitter's popularity makes it a good site to offer real-time commentary on business events, to identify opinion-formers and to make connections by following (and being followed by) others with similar interests or knowledge.

The internet and specifically Web 2.0 technologies offer a plethora of opportunities for networking, but you should pay careful attention to security and privacy issues when networking online. Much information is publicly displayed unless you change the default settings, and some sites regularly change these settings in an attempt to make their user base more attractive to potential advertisers.

Try to:

- search for your real-life contacts on networks and connect to them so that you can find other contacts you have in common

- project a businesslike image (though don't be afraid to comment on the lighter side of events) – you can use multiple profiles on some sites to separate business and personal networks

- use discussion board facilities to raise and comment on topical business issues, and to make others aware of your detailed knowledge and experience

- keep abreast of new networking sites, because the strong competition to be top site can produce useful new web facilities. But remember that even when they are backed by major IT and web providers, new services have relatively few members, so it will take time for them to build a critical mass of potentially useful contacts.

8 Offer help

For many, the most effective form of networking is to give and be useful to others by offering advice, leads, suggestions and ideas. Offer to help if you wish to meet someone again to discuss business. It signals that you are interested in the people themselves and are there to help, rather than just to promote yourself or your products and services.

9 Listen to the contributions of others

Business presentations at meetings can be ideal for picking up possible leads, as people often express their problems to a group, rather than confide only in their business partners. You may also identify competitors who could benefit from a partnership arrangement.

10 Keep records

Set up a database of contacts and take the time to update it regularly. Although you can't take notes while talking to people, it may be possible to jot down a few key words that you can expand on later – after the event, but while your memory is still fresh.

Follow up contacts as appropriate. Regular contact with people will increase the chances that they will remember you and steer business in your direction.

As a manager you should avoid:

- making promises you can't keep, or breaking those you make
- missing opportunities to be useful to others
- forgetting the names of contacts or failing to consider their needs
- retreating into a corner at business meetings
- contacting people only when you want something from them
- overloading your diary with networking events, without considering which will be most useful to you
- mistaking virtual networking for real-life networking, especially if the site allows you to cold-call strangers to make a connection.

Acknowledgements

The Chartered Management Institute (CMI) would like to thank the members of our Subject Matter Experts group for their generous contribution to the development of the management checklists. This panel of over 60 members and fellows of CMI and its sister institute, the Institute of Consulting, draw on their knowledge and expertise to provide feedback on the currency, relevance and practicality of the advice given in the checklists. A full listing of the subject matter experts is available at www.managers.org.uk/policy/subject-matter-experts

This book has been made possible by the work of CMI's staff, in particular Catherine Baker, Piers Cain, Sarah Childs, Michelle Jenkins, Linda Lashbrooke, Robert Orton, Nick Parker, Karen Walsh and not least Mary Wood, the Series Editor. We would also like to thank Stephen Brough and Paul Forty of Profile Books for their support.

The management checklists are based on resources available online at www.managers.org.uk to CMI members to assist them in their work and career development, and to subscribers to the online resource portal ManagementDirect.

Index